Time Statues Revisited

Book Three: Citizenship

Robert F. Morgan

Copyright © 2023 Morgan Foundation Publishers

ISBN:
978-1-885679-22-2 (Paperback)
978-1-885679-27-7 (Ebook)

All rights reserved. No part of this book may be copied or reproduced, stored in a retrieval system, or transmitted in any form, or by any means mechanical, electronic, photocopying, recording or otherwise, without prior written permission of the publisher:

Morgan Foundation Publishers. Email:
morganfoundation@earthlink.net

Web page:
htpp://www.morganfoundationpublishers.com

Time Statues Revisited

Book Three: Citizenship

TABLE OF CONTENTS

Acknowledgements vii
Preview xi
Begin xv

Introduction: Time Statues Revisited 1
CITIZENSHIP 11
Bastille Day 15
Actualizing Democracy 17
Moon over Miami 63
Doc Holliday and ELIZA EARP 67
Conception Opportunity 75
Rise of the Texas Taliban 81
Lifespan of a Cult 87
The Appropriate Place 101
Death Then and Now 103
The Penny Tip 107
After Opening Night in Texas 113
A Fast Descent in Rank 117
A Little Bit More 121
Mister Jim Crow 123
A Cold Case Confession 125

The Time Statue Song Game	127
Boga	137
Columbus Perspective	139
Juneteenth Set Examples	145
Robert Lee Green & Martin Luther King: Revisited	149
Bonus	**163**
Hope for the Next Generation	165
Departures	**171**
Ernst Beier, Ph.D.	173
Pat Norman	179
Hans Toch, Ph.D.	183
References	**187**
Robert F. Morgan	**193**
Other Books by Robert F. Morgan	**195**

Acknowledgements

Thanks first to Asya Blue whose artistry and skills completed the 2021 Time Statues book and now this five book sequel series in 2023.

Otherwise, pretty much the same as in earlier work:

"I thank my past editors from different printing opportunities who encouraged me to write whatever I chose, even if without statistics, graphs, tables, footnotes, or scientific jargon. I was told to just call it *"Commentary"*. Or just write it.

In this I think of Valerie Hearn, with the staff at the *Cambridge University Press*, and Valentine McKay-Riddell, with the staff at the *Four Winds Journal* and the staff at the *Winds of Change Press*.

After decades of publishing about a hundred scientific journal articles and 14 books, it felt good to write freely and outside the confines of professional custom. I thank colleague Charles Tart who shared his own writing strategy: *'Just write what you really want to say. Then, as needed, you can add any citations, references, footnotes, and anything else an editor suggests.'*

Original material in this book is supplemented with my excerpts and illustrations from the *Four Winds Journal*, the Cambridge University Press *Journal of Tropical Psychology*, the *Bulletin of the International Association of Applied Psychology*: Supplement to *Applied Psychology*: *an International Review*, *Trauma Psychology in Context: International Vignettes and Applications from a Lifespan Clinical-Community Psychology Perspective, Opportunity's Shadow and the Bee Moth Effect: When Danger Transforms Community, Unfortunate Baby Names,* and the journal *International Psychology.*

Cited references are found at the end of the book in a consolidated reference section. As to the key mission of understanding the strange world we live in, and what we can do about it, I thank my Guides. Those include Robert Lee Green, Martin Luther King Jr., David Cheek, Michael Knowles, Rollo May, Nathan Hare, Fred Luskin, Sidney Farber, Robert Dattila, or mentors like Stanley Ratner, Bert Karon, Hans Toch, Lois Fisher, Helga Doblin, Cinnamon Morgan, Canadian-born Angel Morgan, plus the multitudes of my friends, teachers, parents and other relatives (my brother Nelson Morgan and forever sister Pat Norman come to mind). Also Michael Butz, Ron Slosky, Len Elkind, and the other thousands of students in six+ decades of teaching who have taught me much in return."

Now: For each of these five new volumes, I have special new appreciation for brilliant editor/inspiration Becky Owl Morgan, Guest contributor Bob Dattila, and the relentless motivating encouragement of Carl Word, Tom Hanrahan, and Dorinda Fox, and Robert Lee Green. Dr. Roland Garcia impressively provided key focused feedback for a much improved reorganization.

Respect is due the earliest *Time Statues* reviewers that mixed insight and comment with their own encouragement: Lois Bridges, Valentine McKay Riddell, Theodore Ransaw, Charles Tart, Hans Toch, and again Robert Lee Green. Great thanks also to Ben Tong for his many contributing illustrations along with insightful historical context. And Jack Hudson for his technical assistance skill.

Some material from my earlier books has been updated, modified, or excerpted here where it necessarily fits to join the original material. Sure, with author permission.

Octogenarian memory can be tricky. You may be curious about anybody deserving to be acknowledged here that I inadvertently left out. Hope not. But an option we can always use is the answers source we learn about all day long on TV commercials.

Ask your doctor.

Preview

ROBERT F. MORGAN

TIME STATUES REVISITED - BOOK THREE: CITIZENSHIP

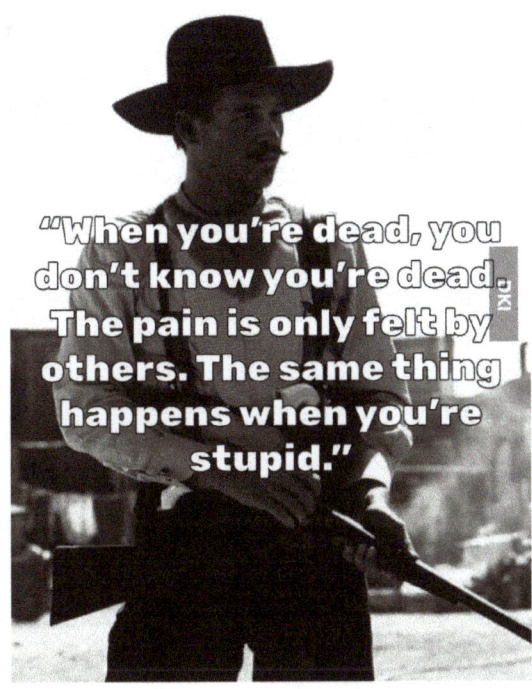

Begin

The Set

This is Book Three of a five book set as follows:

Book One: *On the Job*

Book Two: *Language & Influence*

Book Three: *Citizenship*

Book Four: *Non-Human Relatives*

Book Five: *Human Family*

Optional Music Themes

Just below the chapter title is listed an optional theme, music or video. Some of readers may prefer to listen to this before, during, or after the reading of each chapter. If before, you can play it soundlessly in your mind while reading. You enjoy reading as a kind of movie experience with music enhancing the full experience. This feature is for you.

Other readers may find this a distraction.

The links may have changed since this printing; they may have been infiltrated by multiple commercials.

Or they may just want to avoid any online interference to their reading.

These readers may have grown up in the early or even pre-television generations where radio stories dominated. That required imagination to supply the picture and any music.

For them, we recommend skipping the optional themes entirely.

This omission is for them.

Introduction: Time Statues Revisited

Optional Theme: *Wizards* (Susan Anton) https://www.youtube.com/watch?v=dyOTV8rqM9Q&ab_channel=NatashaDmitriyev

Optional Theme: What Time Is It? (Ken Nordine) https://www.youtube.com/watch?v=1_hdeT4BaRo&ab_channel=KenNordine-Topic

"When I was 5 years old, my mother always told me that happiness was the key to life. When I went to school, they asked me what I wanted to be when I grew up. I wrote down 'happy.' They told me I didn't understand the assignment, and I told them they didn't understand life."

–John Lennon

"Because we are born for a brief span of life, and because this spell of time that has been given to us rushes so swiftly and rapidly that with very few exceptions life ceases for the rest of us just when we are getting ready for it. It is not that we have a short time to live, but that we waste a lot of it. Our lifetime extends amply if you manage it properly."

-Seneca, 65BCE, 2004 AD

Again from Mammaries to Memories

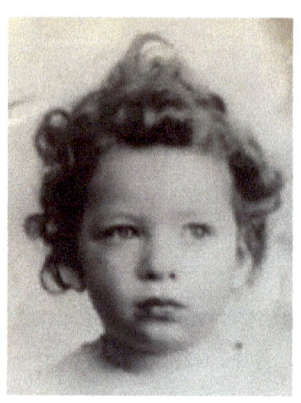

As a pre-school toddler, I already knew that I would grow up to be a writer. Everybody said I was a little Dickens.

Revisit: We were secure and warm, growing in safety. Growing so large that we began to be cramped. Here were the beginnings of desire for a larger apartment. Not to mention that the gentle rocking had become earthquakes.

In that moment or many moments later we first emerged into a new world. A mysterious world. Whirling shapes and colors, rumbling sounds. Made no sense.

We can explore though. Because we had the safety of the cord connecting us still to the warm safety we had left. Our air, our liquid energy. The lifeline is still there.

Hey! It got cut! Gone. Find a new way to breathe! We better figure out this weird place we are in. That's the primary mission. Fast as we can.

It takes a lifetime. And then only a *little* bit understood. Too late to go back to the womb. (On Mother's Day she will emphatically agree.)

The newborn learns to breathe the alien place's air. For energy it can suck nourishment from a giant's huge breast. This perspective might lead to a lifelong craving that will never be fully satisfied. Males seeking ever larger breasts? Females seeking to *have* ever larger breasts? Here for some could be a primal critical period leading to wealthier plastic surgeons and silicon merchants. (What about bottle-fed babies? Maybe alcohol drinks would sell better in baby bottle shaped containers?)

Not us. We moved on. We need not climb the beanstalk to get to the giant. We grew up and *became* the giant.

Whatever else we learned to do, our survival still depends on the mission. To understand this strange world. Remember what we learn. The important stuff.

Time is a place. Each moment is a statue in time, always rooted in that time and that place. Memory allows us to visit them.

After eight decades of this, I have amassed a library of memories. Stacks after stacks of time statues archives.

So much that it can take minutes or more to access just one memory and only with patience. Elders do better at this when we imagine our search as an ordering at a restaurant. Then, usually, it will come. Arriving late? But it will come.

From the viewpoint of age, we can view these memories in their entirety as a grand tapestry. Not necessarily arranged in order, chronologically.

What is a good guiding strategy for navigating these patterns, this treasure in an elder's experience? Maybe it's ones that were meaningful or fun. Sometimes both? Usually based on real past experience. Sometimes not. All of these can be shared.

Now: Well, at least some statues in time can be worth a visit. Or, on reflection, a revisit.

"Peter Rabbit" was a children's play I took my daughters to when they were very young. Peter began each day with great joy for the inevitable adventure. A day for him seemed like a whole season for us humans.

Remember in our own childhood how the beginning of the summer vacation seemed like the opening of endless days? For the shorter lifespan rabbit, each day was like that. It was a revelation for me. A fresh approach.

Jacob von Uexkull first made me aware more fully of the varying perceptual time world of animals:

"Karl Ernst von Baer has made it clear that time is the product of a subject. Time as a succession of moments varies from one Umwelt to another, according to the number of moments experienced by different subjects within the same span of time. A moment is the smallest indivisible time vessel, for it is the expressions of an indivisible elementary sensation, the so-called moment sign. As already stated, the duration of a human moment amounts to 1/18 of a second. Furthermore, the moment is identical for all sense modalities, since all sensations are accompanied by the same moment sign.

The human ear does not discriminate eighteen air vibrations in one second, but hears them as one sound. It has been found that eighteen taps applied to the skin within one second are felt as even pressure.

Cinematography projects environmental motions onto a screen at their accustomed tempo. The single pictures then follow each other in tiny jerks of 1/18 second.

If we wish to observe motions too swift for the human eye, we resort to slow-motion photography. This is a technique by which more than eighteen pictures are taken per second, and then projected at a normal tempo. Motor processes are thus extended over a longer span of time, and processes too swift for our human time-tempo (of 18 per second), such as the wing beat of birds and insects, can be made visible. As slow motion-motion photography slows motor processes down, the time contractor speeds them up. If a process is photographed once an hour and then presented at the rate of 1/18 second, it is condensed into a short space of time. In this way, processes too slow for our human tempo, such as the blossoming of a flower, can be brought within the range of our perception.

The question arises whether there are animals whose perceptual time consists of shorter or longer moments than ours, and in whose Umwelt motor processes are consequently enacted more slowly or more quickly than in ours.

The first experiments of this kind were made by a young German scientist. Later, with the collaboration of another, he studied especially the reaction of the fighting fish to its own mirror image. The fighting fish does not recognize its own reflection if is shown him eighteen times per second. It must be presented to the fighting fish at least thirty times per second. A third student trained the fighting fish to snap toward their food if a gray disc was rotated behind it. On the other hand, if a disc with black and white sectors was turned slowly, it acted as a "warning sign," for in this case the fish received a light shock when they approached their food. After this training, if the rotation speed of the black and white disc was gradually increased, the avoiding reactions became more uncertain at a certain speed, and soon thereafter they shifted to the opposite. This did not happen until the black sectors followed each other within 1/50 second. At this speed the black and white signal had become gray. This proves conclusively that in the world of these fish, who feed on fast moving prey, all motor processes – as in the case of slow-motion photography – appear at reduced speed.

A vineyard snail is placed on a rubber ball which, carried by water, slides under it without friction. The snail's shell is held in place by a bracket. Thus the snail, unhampered by its crawling movements, remains in the same place. If a small stick is then moved up to its foot, the snail will climb up on it. If the snail is given one to three taps with the stick each second, it will turn away, but if four or more taps are administered per second, it will begin to climb onto the stick. In the snail's world a rod that oscillates four times per second has become stationary. We may infer from this that the snail's receptor time moves at a tempo of three to four moments per second. As a result, all motor processes in the snail's world occur much faster than in ours. Nor do its own motions seem slower to the snail than ours do to us." (von Uexkull 1957, Morgan 2005)

Even within our human species great individual variations of time perception exist.

Working with older people, I often saw anxiety about how few years of life it seemed that they had left. I had been working with the full spectrum of human aging and life extension experts, Jim Birren to Timothy Leary. They approached the subject with biology as cause and with psychology as consequence.

What if we reversed the order? What if seniors with the life expectancy of less than a decade approached each day as a season in itself? Instead of ten birthdays and out, why not 3,650 individual seasons to savor, one at a time?

To do this, the senior would need to slow the rocketing passage of time engendered by similar days. Magnified by retirement or illness, one day is much like another. They go by in a flash. This may be comforting but life then goes by quickly. But if each day was differentiated as its own adventure, time will slow down. Life extension occurs experientially. For some, those who accomplished this, they said it helped very much.

We're not rabbits. We live much longer. Or so we can learn to do.

Can each of our days and the moments within them become simply statues of adventure in time?

Building on the earlier *"Time Statues"* book from 2021, once again we come to Einstein and Vonnegut: the temporal community is a place. Each day we finish is fixed for all time. Or is it? We can revisit, this time for new and more challenging ones.

This time we go to the even more interesting ones, although many are protected by metaphorical police tape. Worth the trip? (To help, each chapter begins with a link to a musical theme.)

As we get older, of what we usually regret, it is more often what we did not do than what we did. Either way, a revisit to worthwhile remote events seems worth the return trip. Despite some statues best forgotten.

To navigate effectively in our own normal environment, it is entirely reasonable to consider time as linear and irreversible.

A nonlinear approach will naturally unearth exceptions. The passage through time carries us forward, evolving and adapting. In our nonlinear world, if we are open to it, we can find ways to detour against the current as part of our healthy development. It makes for a richer tapestry than had been expected.

Each moment we live includes our action as our art. Good art or bad art, all that we do sculpts a second-by-second statue to inhabit that time and that place.

The artist continues to live in the limited moments of this lifespan community. Yet the consequences of this art can travel ever further, transcending dangers and obstacles, to shape a better future for our human community.

In this way, we can too.

Star Fleet on a shopping spree.

Time Tip: On the first day of each month, doctors often drop finished patients from their lists. These revisions make that day the very best practical day to try to schedule appointments.

Citizenship

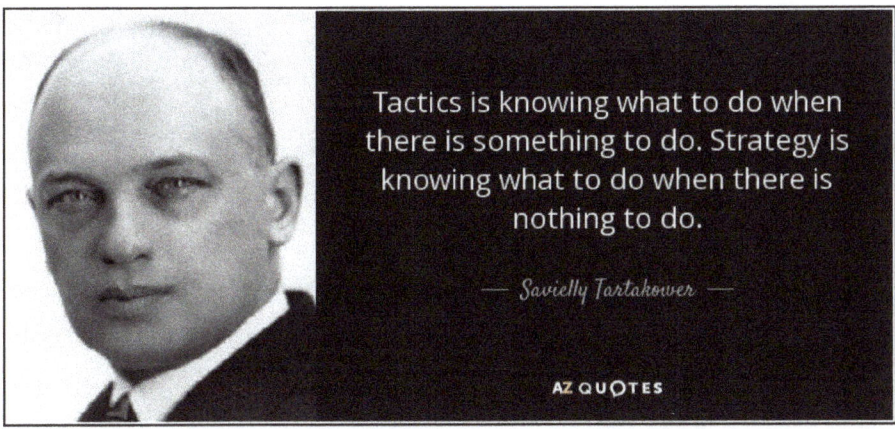

Some running for election can do two or more useful things simultaneously while others cannot do even one good thing simultaneously. Vote accordingly.

When I was stationed in San Antonio for basic training, most of those with me were from the Southern USA. Not surprising since so many military bases were put in the South by a dominant southern Congressional contingent. I learned right away that I was a "Yankee", being from Buffalo, New York. This conversation with a recruit from North Carolina comes to mind.

"If my great grandfather hadn't run out of bullets, you wouldn't be here today!"

"Maybe the key word there is 'run'. Besides, to get my own great grandfather, his bullet would have had to travel to Europe. We just weren't here then."

"They missed out. My people were all from North Carolina and so am I. A proud state!"

"Don't their license plates say 'FIRST IN FLIGHT'?"

"Proud of that too!"

"Meaning the regiment's retreat in the Revolutionary War or the Civil War?"

"Cute. But by the way, we call your 'Civil War' the 'War of Northern Aggression'."

"Aggression to free the slaves."

"Another Yankee lie. The war was about money, about property."

"Sure. The property was people!"*

"That it was. But we were talking about North Carolina."

"A great state. Today we still have great groups based in there."

"The Ku Klux Klan?"

"Sure. And the home of Confederate General Braxton Bragg. Names on one of our bases today."

"Bragg was the kind of general that only rode ahead of his troops in retreat. He even today is considered by many to be the worst most losing Confederate General."

"His name is still on one of our bases."

"Exactly."

Time for a one mile run ended this conversation. We were forewarned by the training sergeant *"Not to toss our cookies"*. No cookies were tossed.

*Note: When George Bush was running for governor of Texas, he was reputed to tell a crowd that the slave owners should have been paid for the *"loss of their property"*. Including, possibly, the Walker side of his family that in fact had owned slaves. (As president, during a visit to Africa, he then denounced slavery.) Amazingly, modern politicians of similar affiliation have repeated the lost property line to their base. As Faulkner said *"The past is never dead. It's not even past"*.

Ziggy

Bastille Day for Caged and Trafficked Immigrant Children

Optional Theme: *La Marseillaise* (Garde Républicaine - Roger Boutry - Choeur De L'Armée Française) **https://www.youtube.com/watch?v=FTIk66b3dds&ab_channel=GardeR%C3%A-9publicaine-RogerBoutry-ChoeurDeL%27Arm%C3%A9e-Fran%C3%A7aise-Mir...-Topic**nal

In France on July 14th their Independence Day holiday celebrates the release of innocent prisoners. It is still cause for celebration. There.

Actualizing Democracy

Optional Theme: *A Change is Gonna Come* (Sam Cooke) https://www.youtube.com/watch?v=fPr3yvkHYsE&ab_channel=EntreCielEtTerre

Said about Richard Nixon: "*If some people were drowning 100 feet off shore, he would throw out 50 feet of rescue rope and claim he had met them halfway*".

My spouse advised me to try acupuncture. I looked for acupuncture on my internal priorities list but, despite being a recognized valid and valuable technique, it was nowhere to be found. Maybe unfairly, I always thought that part of its success might have been motivated by a desire to not be stuck with needles any more. So, I thought: what if she tried it herself and then we looked for improvement measures in me? In this way, my concept of Vicarious Acupuncture was born. (Still waiting for the research to come since she far has decisively declined this invitation to move science forward.)

I found Vicarious Acupuncture as a concept to be very congruent with a contemporary quantum entanglement perspective. This can be far too simply described as: what is done to one of two separate elements impacts the other, with or without any apparent connection and independent of distance.

Second order or vicarious effects in psychology have long been well documented, even if these effects are unexplained, explained, or assumed. Some early examples: Shapiro (1970) demonstrated that the sensitivity training of nurses improved outcomes for their patients. Brandt (1973) found that doing play therapy interventions with parents helped their parenting skills and raised their child's self-concept. This can also apply to the generation of democracy in a system. Chaos theory tells us that even the smallest intervention can have dramatic and systemic consequences, good or bad. Causality is not always clear and is often displaced. But first to definition.

Defining Democracy

"A rose by any other name won't know the difference" (Slattery, 2005)

Eugene Jacobson (1964) defined democracy as *"those most directly affected by a decision, make that decision."* Far from the simplistic concept of "majority rules," Jacobson brought his focus to a just, fair, and specific impact, one that might be considered developmental maturity or psychological health. And it is, in a very good way, contagious.

This can be a very powerful way to look at life's choices.

I taught at San Francisco State University for four years in the early 1970s. When this topic came up, I asked my students in a large class to define democracy. A lively group, some said *"Majority Rules!"* or *"Power to the People!"* These can be very good things, I agreed, but it's not the essence of the idea.

"The opposite of fascism!" somebody said and somebody else yelled *"Democracy is Anti-Fascism!"* (Today named *ANTIFA*.) So I digressed long enough to explore what fascism is: an enmeshment of the biggest corporate business with government such that they are functionally the same thing, consequently only a very few people decide for all the rest, the 1% ruling the 99%. But not enough to define democracy by what it *isn't*.

So time to put some examples on Jacobson's definition.

The early 1970s in San Francisco was a time of freedom, especially for the younger adult generation, in sexual or romantic explorations. The transition was farther along for some than for others. Still, here is the example I gave:

"If this class decided to have a backyard basketball game and divided into two teams of equal numbers. One first choice would be how to tell the two teams apart without uniforms. One of the guys wanted it to be 'Shirts versus skins' where one of the teams played naked from the waist up. Somebody else wanted to take a vote right away where majority rules. Now the males outnumbered the females by a 2 to 1 ratio. While a few males (very few) might not want to be distracted during the game by topless women and a few women (very few) might enjoy being topless as an equity gesture or to gather some interest, suppose that most women in that time would have voted no while most men, of any time, might have voted yes. Majority rule would mean the females, despite being directly affected from an emotional point of view, would lose. That would not be real democracy."

Class discussion followed. Fun for the class. One female student asked me what I would think if she decided to be topless then and there. I said I would know faster if the classroom temperature was too cold.

Hmm. Time to change the subject before we became an indoor Woodstock without music, or a Burning Man gathering without fire (hopefully). Time up. Saved by the bell.

I could well have given this other example of the Jacobson definition from a decade later:

"A president of a small graduate school in Palo Alto wanted to avoid lawsuits from students or their families over sexual hook-ups with faculty. He took the initiative to appoint a "Presidential Commission" to decide on an ethical policy for student-faculty dating. To cheat and make sure he got the outcome he wanted, a prohibition, he populated his commission entirely with older female graduate students. To his chagrin, their deliberations resulted in a DEMAND that students, as legal adults, date anybody they chose, especially including any faculty. The president charged me, as his Academic Vice President, with bringing the faculty together to come up with their own policy. This I did. The American Association of University Professors (AAUP) already had a policy on this: no dating within your discipline or major but freedom anywhere else. The essence of this was to avoid a conflict of interest where a supervisor or person of coercive authority over a student could not really have an equally free consent from the subordinate student. One of the faculty suggested that any of them having had sex with a student should just leave the room when faculty were discussing that student's progress. Another asked what would happen if everybody

left? And so it went. We finally agreed that sex with a faculty member actively supervising a student, class or in any other way should be prohibited. Otherwise the decision of the female students on their Presidential Commission would be honored. Eventually, following the AAUP, any core or fulltime faculty of this single discipline graduate school would also be prohibited from dating a student. Since everybody was affected by this choice, with consultation from both groups, the decision stood. In time it was enforced and a few faculty lost their jobs. (Of course that very President had married one of his own students. No consequences for him)."

Maybe not the best example after all. Though I enjoyed the memory. Let's get back to applying the Jacobson definition of democracy.

Of course, democracy is not a panacea. While creating a very healthy psychological atmosphere, some human applications would not work well. A felon about to be sentenced for a violent crime will most directly be impacted by that decision, but that decision is better left to the judge or jury. Nor could a military function as a complete democracy when it is fundamentally designed to be hierarchical.

A toddler heading for a hazardous crossing:

Definitely needs a parent to intervene.

Still, democracy in most other cases is usually the most successful and peaceful way for decisions to be made. And should be encouraged. National movements toward this all across the globe should be actualized.

Being Inductive

Every community has its own collective personality. Rigid adherence to predetermined expectation may be misleading at best. Gathering data first, combing the literature, observing carefully and systematically can provide a more inductive approach to a better outcome.

Democracy is change that is by its nature inductive; in hierarchical systems it operates from the bottom up.

Now applying a good theory is very practical. But even these theories can be modified in unexpectedly helpful ways when those most directly affected provide feedback. How about an example from education?

Example from Education
I thought I made a mistake but I was wrong

Building on the decades of work by pioneers like A.S. Neill (Neill 1978; Neill & Lamb 1995, Reich 1981) and Jonathon Kozol (1967, 1985, 2006), Dr. Thomas Toy and I evaluated a 3-month program in which high school children tutored grade school children one-to-one a few hours each week during study hall. While the grade school children learned twice as much as their controls, the high school tutors learned three times as much as *their* controls.

We recommended an Educational Cooperative model where each child briefly tutored a younger one on a regular basis each week (Morgan & Toy, 1970, 1974). Such a model substitutes generational collaboration for antagonism, not only between children but between the teenage tutors and their teachers. The threat of their being embarrassed by not being able to explain what they were teaching to the younger children was reduced since the tutors now chose to learn the material to 100% mastery before they tried to teach it. We predicted that, in addition to enhanced test scores, bullying would decline and disciplinary problems for tutors would decrease. This occurred but was not really noticed by most of the high school teachers.

When I prevailed on Tom Toy, my graduate student at the time, to do the extra work of evaluating the tutors as well as the outcome measures for the younger students they tutored, it was because of my pre-existing theory. I believed that this antagonistic gap between adolescent students and their teachers would be far less combative once these adolescents experienced the role of teacher themselves. In this way they would begin to see their teachers as masters of the very educational skills they too needed to succeed in their mission. To test this hypothesis, I predicted the tutors would also improve, possibly even more than those they tutored. When this occurred, to the surprise of many, I considered my theory validated.

I met with the adult teachers and shared the study results, suggesting they use an Educational Cooperative Model (Morgan & Elkind 1972, Morgan, 2012). In this model the child's learning was enhanced by teaching younger children one-to-one, at least a few hours each week.

My role identification theory led me to suggest the young tutors should even get a small paycheck, just like an adult teacher, and even be on a first name basis with their adult teachers.

This did not go over well. One teacher proclaimed that he had as a child sat in the very classroom he was teaching in now. Instead now that he was the teacher and not the student, he demanded to be called by his formal name. If not, he would feel he had made no progress, that he would lose control or dominance over the children in his class. I pointed out that he was much bigger than the children in his classroom now. No luck. The teachers wanted the gap to continue.

At this point I added a key component to the study, one I have urged adding to every one of my 121 supervised doctoral dissertations since. Post-study participant feedback. We decided to meet with the participants directly affected by the study, the adolescent tutors, to discuss why their improvement had surpassed the children they had taught.

Tom Toy and I met with them as a group, shared the study results, and asked them for comment. The feedback was not what I expected. They had a better explanation than my role identification theory.

In the United States, the mass production group-in-a-classroom education model prevails almost completely over individualized instruction. There a scale chosen to measure success is a letter grade and percent score approach. In that, a perfect score would be 100%. A, B, C, D, F are the usual letters used with A the highest, and F the failing grade. In Singapore and many other British-style systems, letter grades give way to "Distinction" (70%) or "High Distinction" (80%), also based on a percentage where 100% is a perfect score. In the USA system, typically 90% success earns the A, 80% the B, 70% the C, 60% the D (barely passing), and 0-59% an F or failing grade. (Other countries can have far different interpretations of percentage; more about that later.)

Our cohort of tutors pointed out that even if they had earned grades of A through all their years of school, they had earned them with a 90% or so, leaving a mastery gap of up to 10% in every course.

Those getting B or C grades had content gaps of up to 30%. Over the years, these gaps of missed learning accumulated. But then, in our study, they had no desire as a tutor to be embarrassed by any mistakes made in front of the younger children they taught. So they learned 100% of what they were about to teach before they taught it. In this way, they had discovered the mastery method of learning by teaching and it immediately enhanced their performance in their own classroom courses.

Their learning by teaching theory was far more valid than my own role identification one. It identified learning by teaching as a key education intervention. As good teachers know for themselves. Sharing this technique with students is a great next step.

Also clear was that, whenever possible, it is always important to share a study's results with participants for their feedback. This is not only respectful and just, but often essential to understanding the results. And it actualizes democracy.

The Keller mastery method (Morgan & Toy 1974; Sherman 1974) built on this model over the years, primarily in higher education. Today's educational milieu could benefit by a fresh look at the Educational Cooperative method in which teaching is a primary method for learning.

The Singapore Disruption

You recall that in Singapore and many British systems, success is measured by *"Distinction"* (70%) or *"High Distinction"* (80%), based on a percentage where 100% is a perfect score. When I was a Visiting Professor at an Australian university campus in Singapore, faculty were actually handed a written notice by the CEO that mandated not more than 5-10% of students in any class receive "distinction" or "high distinction" grades. Psychology doctoral programs in the USA instead typically mandate that students achieving anything less than a grade of 80% (B) can be dropped from the program. At my Singapore campus though, everything at 80% or above was *high* distinction.

Rather than doing a grading curve, I just told the students that their grade would be whatever they earned (0-100%). Further, I would do all in my power to assist them to learn all of the material needed to master the course (Mastery Learning). Since students in the Honours and Clinical Psychology programs were already highly selected for motivation/ability/knowledge, most did well. By USA graduate standards, there would have been some grade distribution: As and Bs mostly. But by that university's standards, when all or nearly all the students achieved scores of mastery of at least 70% of the course material, I naturally awarded them their "distinction" grades. This, it turned out, was apparently a social embarrassment to the university administration. Even in my one undergraduate Honours class, of 23 students only one failed the course, while all the rest did very well. In a "distinguished" or "high distinguished" way. In many countries that would be expected, possibly celebrated, but then and there it led to much fury and consternation.

Once grades were in, the faculty member in charge of the Honours program sat in my office with tears of rage running down her cheeks. She said I had used up the 5% of high distinction grades allotted to her program in a single class. I realized then that, from her point of view, it was like I had arrived early to her picnic and eaten all the food.

Then came the administrative response to my Honours and clinical psychology students receiving non-curved grades. There was a review, all the way by technology from the Australian main campus. In this proceeding, the demand was for me to justify why my grades were not in line with other faculty. An official proclaimed that "it could only be grade inflation." Although comparison across different courses in different countries with different instructors with varying students in each class was not logical, my own students were objectively graded on a wide variety of written and performance standards in each class. They were actually some of the best motivated and educated students I have ever taught anywhere. They had earned their grades.

The pre-determined curve was an abusive application of theory. I had instead chosen a more inductive approach, one dependent on the performance of those most directly impacted.

In the exchange with the perturbed administrators, I wondered if my teaching experience (50 years then) might have made a difference. Instead, I then asked them: what level of mastery would they accept for their personal physician? Would he or she be considered proficient ("distinction") and safe if they had only learned 70% of what a physician should know? I suggested that we should have our clinical psychology graduates do their best to reach 100%, or as close as they can get, and not feel smug about the graduation of clinical students with only 70% of the essential knowledge or skills required for treating patients successfully.

Despite their administration, some of my Australian faculty counterparts expressed interest in this mastery learning, seeing that it had promise to enhance our ultimate professional mission of service to our patients. In its purest form, mastery learning steps away from a fixed time frame of academic quarters or terms: students do not move onto the next step until they reach complete (100%)

demonstrated understanding of the step they are on. Some finish faster, some need more time. At their university, a modified version might just ditch the forced curve and attempt as close to mastery as possible in the time allowed, as I had done. One could also drop grades entirely and just use credit/no credit with a narrative (often done at some University of California campuses and many other university systems in the world).

When they were in elementary school, my daughters were once both put in a "Gifted Class" for high IQ children. Unfortunately they forgot to hire a gifted teacher to run the class. The non-gifted teacher immediately instituted a curved grading system yielding hierarchical grades by the end of the first term. A student with an IQ of 130 would fail the class if there were other students with an IQ of 140+. Some very bright and motivated students had their first failure experience in school despite excellent work, work just not as excellent as their competitors. A few lost interest in school. My own children did well, but another very bright child dropped out and never went back.

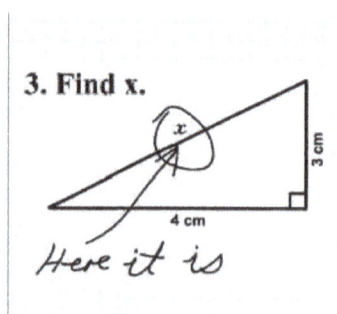
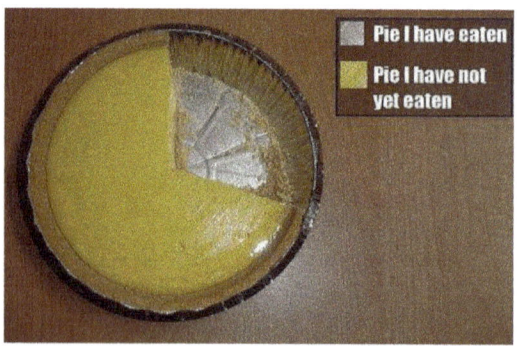

In rare occasions, I've never had difficulty, as faculty or administration, in providing a failing grade or facilitating departure of a student who, despite every reasonable opportunity, earned this outcome. Mostly though, I have had the pleasure of seeing substantial learning take place with the right set and setting. I do suspect the grading curve approach may well be one major component in reducing many a university's retention. If followed, it elevates the self-worth of the top 5-10% while diminishing that of the remaining majority. This outcome fits only when the destructive goal is perpetuating the hierarchical antithesis to actualizing democracy.

Education at its best requires a cooperative cohort to develop. Not a cutthroat competition reducing learning levels all around to create superior and inferior status hierarchies. But actualizing democratic alternatives is not universally popular. And so there and then my Visiting Professorship came to an end.

Other Examples from Adult Literacy and Rehabilitation

Such a principle was also practiced effectively in Martin Luther King's Adult Literacy programs in Chicago, the only federally funded programs given directly to a Civil Rights organization. Here the tutors providing one-to-one instruction, a key success component too long ignored in the mass production education model, had the prior experience of graduating the program, no longer illiterate. As part of their teaching role, they wrote their own community-friendly curriculum (Woolman, 1967). I was a psychologist brought in to evaluate its success. Success was defined as 6th grade level literacy and holding a subsequent job. I was delighted to see more than 98% success. A competing program run by the mayor had less than 10% success.

(Note: Woolman also used his technique to move integrated childhood education forward. He used his focus on individual tutoring along with meaningful locally-generated content (Lazar *et al*, 1982,

Consortium of Longitudinal Studies, 1983). Not only was this ***"Operational Context Training"*** used to effect in Dr. King's adult literacy programs, but it was actually an impetus for desegregating public schools in the Southern USA. Woolman would allow use of his technique, the one achieving Grade 6 Reading Level in a few months, *only* for grades K-6 schools that accepted African American children. The fear to compete engendered in segregationist school boards by these 5-12-year-old African American children, who now read extremely well, was sufficient for them to open up their school system to children of all colors. Of course, recent educational dogma focusing entirely on mass education techniques has eclipsed this approach and consigned individual instruction to isolated special education. In fact, if re-awakened, it could be faster, cheaper, and transform the community in a generation.)

Our education is provided on the cheap and profoundly under-funded. Consequently, the individual is lost in favor of group education. But entire communities can have their survival skills upgraded by more effective education of their children, both as to content and learning to learn, critical thinking, and comprehension of the culture.

Illiteracy is a major and often overlooked causative feeder for our prison system. Educational transformation is cheaper.

Yet even prison can be transformational given these principles. Hans Toch's years of work on inmate governance and humanistic corrections (Toch 1980, 1995, 1997, 2017) presents a valuable educational cooperative model employing therapeutic community empowerment in a highly challenging setting. The most powerful post-prison community success of this model that I have found has definitely been the self-reliant entrepreneurial Delancey Street Foundation, where ex-convicts live together, run businesses and move to self-sufficiency, even building their own housing.

The DELANCEY STREET FOUNDATION

Dr. Mimi Silbert is the founder and President of the *Delancey Street Foundation* headquartered in San Francisco, California. As a matter of fact, for 50 years now, *Delancey Street*, considered the nation's leading self-help residential education center for former substance abusers and ex-convicts, has transformed the lives of over 11,000 graduates into productive members of the community.

At slightly under five feet tall, Silbert slays her challenges head on. She does this by implementing the principle of helping others help themselves. *Delancey Street* was named after the section of New York where immigrants assembled at the turn of the century. Silbert, a criminologist and psychologist, modeled *Delancey Street* after her own extended family in an immigrant neighborhood of Boston. In 1971, Silbert, along with former felon John Maher, started the program for ex-cons with a $1,000 loan from a loan shark. They started small with only four drug addicts as residents. Today there are about 1,000 residents located throughout the country. There are now five facilities, including locations at their San Francisco headquarters, Los Angeles, New Mexico, New York, and North Carolina. Dr. Mimi Silbert explained:

"Our population ranges in age from 18 to 68; approximately 1/4 are women; 1/3 African American, 1/3 Hispanic, and 1/3 Anglo. The average resident has been a hard-core drug addict for ten years and has been in prison four times. Approximately seventy (70%) come from the courts, and about thirty percent (30%) have been homeless prior to entering Delancey Street.

Despite the violent and criminal backgrounds of our residents, there has never been one arrest in the 25 years we have operated, and gang members once sworn to kill one another are now living in integrated dorms and working together cooperatively and non-violently.

Although the average resident is functionally illiterate and unskilled when entering Delancey Street, all residents receive a high school equivalency and are trained in three different marketable job skills before graduating. The minimum stay at Delancey Street is two years; the average stay is four years. During that time, residents learn not only academic and vocational skills, but also the interpersonal, social survival skills, along with the attitudes, values, sense of responsibility, and self-reliance necessary to live in the mainstream of society drug-free, successfully, and legitimately.

Over 11,000 men and women have graduated into society as taxpaying citizens leading successful lives—including lawyers, truck drivers, sales people, various medical practitioners, realtors, mechanics, contractors, and even a member of the San Francisco Board of Supervisors, the President of the San Francisco Housing Commission, a deputy coroner, and a deputy sheriff.

We have accomplished this at no cost to the taxpayer or the client. One of the most unique features of Delancey Street is that we have never accepted any government funds, nor do we have any staff. The entire organization is run by its residents in the process of changing their lives. The foundation supports itself primarily through a number of training schools which provide vocational skills to all the residents, and which also generate the Foundation's income through pooling the monies earned. Training schools include a Moving and Trucking School, a Restaurant and Catering Service, a Print and Copy Shop, Retail and Wholesale Sales, Paratransit Services, Advertising

Specialties Sales, Christmas Tree Sales and Decorating, and an Automotive Service Center, among others.

In 1990, the residents built from the ground up their very own block, sometimes referred to as the Embarcadero Triangle, along the breathtaking San Francisco Bay waterfront. The monstrous task—a 325,000-square-foot, four-story building—was built at about half the cost of the current $30 million appraisal. Everyone worked together with pride. Over 300 formerly unemployed drug addicts, homeless people and ex-felons build their very own 177-unit Mediterranean-style masterpiece.

The Delancey Street Foundation testifies to what can be accomplished when the disadvantaged of society are afforded opportunity. Delancey Street has been featured on 60 Minutes, 20/20, Oprah Winfrey Prime Time Special, PARADE Magazine, People Magazine, and Time Magazine, to name only a few. The Delancey Street principle holds that ordinary people can transform extraordinary—even impossible—dreams into reality by pooling their resources, supporting one another, and living lives of purpose and integrity." (Bickford, 2002)

Violence Prevention and Interviews from Inductive Cohorts

I just received and read a fairly recent (2017) book from Hans Toch: *Violent Men: An Inquiry into the Psychology of Violence, 25th Anniversary Edition*. This is an intervention book. Nothing in print better illustrates how applied psychology can turn inductive data into democratic interventions.

Professor Toch wrote a jacket quote for me once. It was for my *Iatrogenics Handbook: A Critical Look at Research & Practice in Helping Professions* (Morgan 2005). This was a collaborative book that explored ways people can be hurt by health or educational professionals in the process of being helped, and how to prevent this. ("Iatrogenic" is a term sometimes boiled down to "the doctor's mistakes," now a top cause of mortality.) With a concise and witty scalpel, the final line of the Toch quote was for me the most memorable: *"If the shoe fits, it will hurt."* (See "Departures" section at the end of this book.)

This book of his, at a distance, may well be mistaken for a simple reprint of his original from 25 years ago, possibly with a new preface. Not at all. New sections and authors are added. I liked the risk assessment one, among others. This edition kept the original 1992 essence but, by adding fresh material, explodes into the current era with a mixture of new insights, useful contemporary applications, and compelling evidence on how prophetic the original book turned out to be. And 25 years of even more experience for the author didn't hurt. Brilliance becomes wisdom. Humor still brightens the reading, also illuminating the reader.

See. Hans could have said all those words in my last paragraph so much more concisely.

Hmm. I can try. Great read. Well worth the time in our finite life. Choices must be made and this book was a really good one. How's that? In considering his book, I am reminded of the two best interview questions I have experienced in my own more than half-century as a psychologist. At least the two that come to mind.

(1) McMaster

At the onset of the 1970s, a group of McGill University psychiatrists moved from Montreal to run the McMaster University department of psychiatry and its clinic in so innovative a manner that it would be considered progressive even today. They had a successful rehabilitation program focused from the beginning on career/job development for their patients.

Since I was finishing a stretch as a Visiting Professor elsewhere in Canada, I was intrigued when they asked me to come give a talk. On arrival, they told me that they were considering an offer for me to join them. So now it was a job interview. One of them would sit in on my talk. The rest would be busy during that time contacting my references, but ones from a very special list. This list would be based on the question: *"Of the people you have worked for, which ones would give you the worst reference?"* Amused and fascinated, I fully complied. I had already been out in the field long enough to earn a few such antagonistic reviews. After my talk, which apparently they liked, they asked me to join them. As to the calls to the hostile referees, they concluded: *"What they hate about you is exactly what we are looking for."*

Reading the newest Toch contribution, his successful pursuit of this challenging subject while surmounting obstacles along the way, is exactly what we have been looking for.

(2)Therapeutic Community

Also in the mists of the past, I was invited to audition as consultant to a San Diego therapeutic community program for patients diagnosed with schizophrenia. This too was a very innovative and successful program. Employing what we now know to call "Tochian" participatory methodology, the inhabitants had a strong say in the way they were treated. This included a pass or fail interview with me before I could become their consultant. After introductions all around, I was only asked one question: *"What is it that you do that gets you in the most trouble?"*

I just opened my mouth to learn what would come out and it was *"My sense of humor."* They liked that. Agreed that was often their downfall too. I passed the test.

Professor Toch's work always has had this key ingredient. An essential unrelenting sense of humor. Also, you learn something new and useful in every chapter.

Actualizing Democracy in Clinical Psychology

Psychotherapy includes active listening, behavioral pattern recognition, ethical and legal context, compassionate empathy, inductive detective collaboration, diagnostic experience, follow-up consumer feedback, and interventions including intuitive humor and advocacy that actualizes democracy. The last has implications for international applied psychologists as it is explored here.

A Tale of Two Clinics

Some universities compete primarily and excessively with another one nearby. In my pre-doctoral training years at Michigan State University, for example, I learned that its competing institution, the University of Michigan, would loan its bound dissertations to any other university *except* Michigan State. This was a rivalry that went beyond football. The rationale (rationalization) was that the driving distance was too close to justify loans, although closer institutions had no such problem.

In the state of Alaska, two major public universities had such rivalry. To attempt a bridge across this divide, the leaders of the system funded a joint program to train much needed community-clinical psychologists. The University of Alaska program brought faculty from the Anchorage and Fairbanks campuses together to train the first cohorts of what looked to be an exciting program. Faculty tele-conferences were held regularly in real time with split screen technology. (Today I would want virtual reality capacity.) Student cohorts were brought together as often as the forbidding geography and climate allowed. Indigenous healers, one a psychologist, were consultants and co-faculty. There was a strong research granted base and ongoing separate Clinical and Community practicum experiences.

I was brought in to the Fairbanks campus to teach and supervise the new training clinic. Time to actualize democracy in the training?

The clinic had six meeting rooms, a record room, a reception desk, and my office. White noise machines were outside each meeting room door to maintain auditory confidence. An indigenous ceremony graced the clinic on opening day. There were six interns, all excellent and mature graduate students, every one dedicated to the community.

One, an Alaska Native, candidly said she did not anticipate liking individual psychotherapy in the clinic but would do it as well as she could so she might return to her community with the PhD credential and better help them. (She did her best, which was superb, and in the end decided she loved clinical work because *"I was honored to hear their stories,"* and she did help them make their next stories better.)

I assigned each intern to a specific room, with a request that they decorate it in a way that would enhance their work, create a safe and comfortable environment for their community clients, and express their own personality. This they did, creatively and effectively. Each room had a strong but comfortable setting, one individualized to the choices of the intern. To better prepare for their eventual post-graduate career doing this sort of work, we had business cards made for each of them. Every week I did individual supervision of cases with each intern based in part on the video-taped sessions with a camera in every room. We also did a group supervision and another group meeting to share decisions on clinic function. Each client filled out a very brief evaluation after each session (satisfaction: yes or no, and a space for comment) and as a follow-up after conclusion of their intern experience. Based on this, the clients were very happy with the service and seemed to resolve their issues to lasting satisfaction. The Fairbanks clinical faculty were happy with the clinic and the Fairbanks campus students were pleased to tell the Anchorage campus students how pleased they were with their experience.

Which may have contributed to some problems. There were two program heads with equal authority, one for each campus. My program leader arranged a touring visit to my clinic for his Anchorage counterpart, and for me to make a subsequent visit to her clinic there.

The Anchorage campus program head was met with the traditional great welcome and, following a meal with faculty, she began the clinic tour. As we went through each aspect and met each smiling intern, her demeanor soured. She was polite but clearly unhappy. No concerns were expressed, even after my request for criticism. This I didn't understand until my later visit to her campus.

My wife and I arrived but nobody was there to meet us. We took a taxi to the campus but the head of the program was busy and said we should go to visit the clinic on our own. So we did.

In Anchorage it was a top-down hierarchical approach. The psychology doctoral students were on the bottom of this ladder. The clinic there belonged to another program and the doctoral students were sandwiched in as openings occurred. The supervision was done by a central monitor but individual supervision of cases was unsatisfying, said the students we spoke with. The rooms were identical and Spartan. No business cards. No client evaluation opportunity or follow-up. Despite this, they did use the same progressive technology that we did in Fairbanks, albeit in their own way.

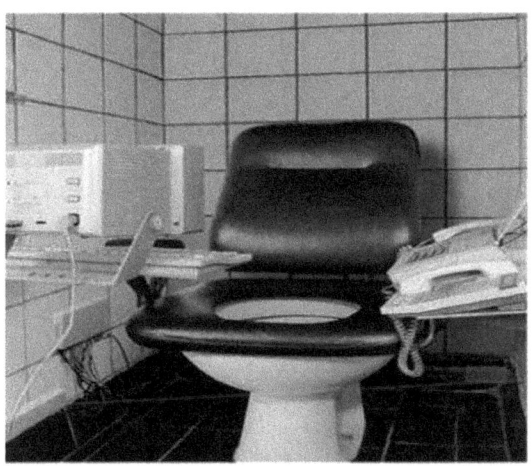

The doctoral students available said their program head was unhappy with the "coddling" I was giving to the Fairbanks students. Some had asked to transfer to our Fairbanks clinic practicum as they liked our model much better. But these requests were denied.

Looking for something positive, I asked how their community practicum was going. They liked this experience, but here too there was a fundamental distinction in perspective between campuses. The community practicum in Fairbanks defined community as indigenous native people. In Anchorage, the community practicum has mostly defined community as local organizations, businesses, and government entities. This all counted as advocacy and was undoubtedly useful experience. But not quite what our Fairbanks faculty, me included, thought of as Alaska's greatest community opportunity and need.

When it came time for me to leave, a cohort of doctoral students from both campuses petitioned the program to keep me on permanently. The petition was taken under advisement but, nearly a decade later, it is still apparently being studied. The intern students we stayed in touch with did graduate and went on to have successful careers as psychologists, most staying in Alaska. They continued our practice of treating their own clients and students with respect. Short term or long term, we can only provide educational oases in time, transient but beneficial while they last. And again, actualizing democracy in hierarchical systems is not always welcome. To say the least. Those who choose to actualize democracy always keep their bags packed.

Three years later I developed a similar clinical psychology practicum for interns in a Singapore clinic. It too was much appreciated by their community clients.

(Note: When I used to site visit community Clinics, if they had no client evaluation feedback in place, I would do a telephone survey of past clients. Typical satisfaction percentage averaged about 60%. Then when I convinced the Clinic to give clients a written feedback opportunity, subsequent year telephone survey satisfaction jumped to an average of about 90%. Just asking people if they are satisfied increased satisfaction. Businesses have become aware of this and successful ones routinely ask their customers for feedback. Having a say in what affects us directly, even post hoc, is actualized democracy.)

Election Systems That Actualize Democracy
Vote Ranking

The American Psychological Association initiated a vote transfer system for elections. With multiple candidates, the one receiving the fewest votes is dropped and those who voted for that candidate have their second choice vote counted. This continues until a single candidate is left and that person wins. This method allows voters to rank their choices, allowing more of their decisions to count. In contrast, systems requiring a single non-ranked vote may elect a poor candidate most voters don't want by splitting their votes among several excellent candidates. Priority ranking votes can be the future in any actualized democracy. Some states, Alaska for one, are already voting in this way.

Note: One of the two first free-standing professional schools of psychology campuses began in San Francisco in 1971. Its 13 founding core faculty gathered to elect a representative by paper ballot. Although we had just met, it became clear that these psychologist pioneers were natural leaders. So much so that I suggested any traditional vote procedure might wind up undecided or unimpressive since my colleagues would likely just vote for themselves. After laughing agreement, I was challenged to recommend an alternative.

I said it might be better to vote for two candidates instead of one, a first and second choice. In this way anybody or everybody who wanted to vote for their self could do exactly that and we still would have enough second choices to get a majority. This we did. Sure enough, each of us had received at least one vote. Possibly because I had suggested this ad hoc voting system, most put my name down as a second choice, giving me the majority. This is how I became a

Dean in my first of four years at the California School of Professional Psychology. Democracy works in mysterious ways.

Belling the Cat

Even a stopped clock is right twice a day.

When I joined the faculty at a Pacific Rim university, they were profoundly and justifiably unhappy with their President. These faculty were generally quite gifted and articulate but rightly concerned about losing their jobs in any direct confrontation with this administrator. So it was that I was asked by the faculty union to do the formal evaluation. With my faculty team, we chose not to pinpoint the President alone. Instead we evaluated all the top administrators, including Vice Presidents and Deans. Again, the "Should this person be continued in their position" question was asked. With one exception, the administration received varying levels of majority confidence (although the comments were not universally friendly). The exception of course was the unpopular President, an outcome that had a vast majority (90%+ as I recall) wanting this President to resign. Which he refused to do.

Eventually the university's accreditation body intervened at our request. This led to the resignation of the President and the formation of a Faculty Senate. There I continued my charge with a faculty team that conducted an annual evaluation of the administration, Deans through President. Again it was not over-complicated. There were no hard to interpret nine-point scales. Every faculty member had the written opportunity to recommend or not recommend the continuation of their top supervisors. The yes/no recommendation was again coupled with an opportunity to comment. These results were tabulated and shared with faculty and all the administrative supervisors. Nearly all of them were recommended to continue although comments for improvement were more balanced this time between applause and criticism. Faculty morale rose even higher. The annual evaluation system became embedded in the Senate bylaws.

I did note that the Board of Directors did an annual evaluation of the President. The Board Chair liked my idea of using the evaluation from faculty as a key component of their assessment, further agreeing that annual continuation should be contingent on a majority vote of confidence from faculty.

(Note: When it came time to elect faculty to their Senate, they were voted for in their respective schools within the university. This led to some concern over partisanship. I suggested that we divide the total number of faculty by the number of Senators to be elected and use that number for a petition process. If, for example, the number resulting from the division was 25, then a Senator would be elected automatically with a petition signed by any 25 faculty, local or not. But no faculty member could sign more than one petition. I really liked this transparent process idea. Nobody else seemed to. Never mind.)

In earlier decades, going a rung lower on academic hierarchy, I joined the movement leaders in the service of having students in higher education evaluate their instructors at the close of each course, today a common event. This proved harder to do with teachers of children in public schools. I did enjoy suggesting to teachers of five-year-old children that they let their students give *them* a letter grade in each report card. Little applause from teachers for this.

As an administrator in many different capacities, I always had the people I supervise do an annual evaluation of me (stay or go, with comment) in addition to the one-to-one mutual supervision feedback most organizations now require. This is still not a universally used procedure.

At the very beginning of that time I was a Dean at the California School of Professional Psychology, San Francisco, I initiated a process where the students evaluated everybody who worked there, receptionist to CEO (stay or go, with comment) and the results were distributed to everybody on campus. I always promised I would step down as a supervisor if I did not have the confidence of the majority of my supervisees. I then had this done by students for their faculty instructor in each course (satisfied or not, with comment).

This was met with resistance from some senior faculty. *"If my students don't like my teaching, should I just shoot myself?"* said one. I said *"That or just improve the teaching—your choice."* Again all results were tabulated, typed and distributed with no screening. And here I found a limit. One student in one of my classes put in his evaluation: *"Morgan's teaching is fine but the class would go a lot better if Gene XXXX had a giant cork put in his mouth."* Gene's actual full name was used. A former professional football player, Gene was quite vocal in class. He read the part of the evaluation about himself in our class for the first time. Well, he took it well for a few seconds, smiled, then turned red in the face and moved fast against the student he knew had written this. I barely prevented violence in the classroom.

After that, evaluators were warned that comments about other students would be removed, although anything about the teacher or administrative staff would remain. That worked much better. Pure democracies may at time require some focus.

In a recent year, I was invited to give a talk at a private Louisiana university. The state had recently changed the requirement for their endowed Chairs for Distinguished Professors. The recipients now, immediately, had to be demonstrably distinguished by publication and experience. The university had up to this time been using these positions to hire new PhD graduates, who then taught the courses no other faculty wanted to teach. Now they had some interest in my coming there to work as well as to speak, lest they lose the funding for the endowed Chair.

Before I could give my talk, I was scheduled for a two-day marathon, early morning to late evening, of meetings with all levels of university inhabitants. The students were interested and interesting as ever, the staff engaged, and the President, a man with impressive business and legal experience, cordial.

The faculty, though, were unhappy. The new President was liked well enough, but not his actions. These generally moved decision-making away from faculty. Decisions that directly impacted their work were now made at a variety of administrative levels. While this was congruent with the state's political leadership philosophy, it did strike the faculty as a substantial shift from their prior, more progressive role, one providing a sense of ownership in the organization, a somewhat actualized democracy.

By the end of the second day, I was exhausted. But it was time for my talk and the room was full. Faculty, staff, administration, students—every seat filled. I had planned to talk about educational group interventions in a state hospital, in the Peace Corps, in prisons. But as I stood to begin, I decided to talk about actualizing democracy, with abundant faculty examples.

The faculty and staff seemed fascinated, administrators appalled. By the time I was done, I had a feeling my welcome from administration had evaporated. The message waiting on my phone when I returned to my home state that night confirmed this.

(Note: For international perspective, my talk had included some linguistic examples of cultural double entendre. The biggest laugh came when I shared that the word "lawyer" in Canada's Nova Scotia and parts of the British Empire is pronounced "liar." I suspect all were not equally amused.)

Time Release Impact

In an earlier decade, I had interviewed at another Louisiana university, this time a well-known public one. The position was that of Department Chair in a large psychology department. Their major interest was in gaining accreditation for their doctoral program, something I have done many times over the years. I gave a talk and met with the faculty. Following an hour of questions and conversation, they shared that I was the last of three candidates being interviewed. Then their Dean would receive their rankings and recommendations of the candidates. I asked "Who would make the actual hiring decision?" Apparently nobody had asked that there before and the faculty response was surprised enthusiasm. I was told that this was an important question. I agreed. Discussion ensued.

I left my very friendly welcome from the faculty to meet with the Dean. He was primarily interested in a successful accreditation effort and suggested that my past success in this made my hiring something I should plan on. My wife and I were given plenty of time to look at housing and imagine a life there.

Once we were home, the days and weeks went by without a decision. I now and then called their hiring office but was told to be patient as the position was still unfilled and I was still a top candidate. Months went by and the seasons changed. Same response.

A year later I took another job, leaving the Louisiana mystery unsolved.

Then, much later, we by chance met some of the same Louisiana faculty at a dinner. Mystery solved. Turned out that the faculty had wanted to take no chances and just sent the Dean one name, mine, and not the three candidate names the Dean had expected. The Dean let them know that he thought I would be fine for the position but he found their approach to be insubordinate, to him a more important issue. The Dean demanded that the faculty recommend all three candidates to him as the hiring decision was his alone to make. The faculty said they were unanimous in their choice and the decision should be theirs. The Dean said he would approve no decision until the faculty recommended all three candidates. The faculty declined. Impasse. The position remained unfilled.

Eventually many of the faculty relocated to another university. Once there, hiring and other decisions directly affecting them returned.

(Note: I have been told I have "time-release humor" meaning it takes a while to get it, but the time-release impact of certain questions and discussions suggests we need some patience in assessing change. I have also been enjoying doing some 40+ year follow ups with former psychotherapy clients. Valuable lifespan feedback.)

Rights are Recognized

As shared in an earlier chapter: A priest from the university philosophy department, Father Angelus, arose and said in a voice that shook the rafters: *"Thank you Father President. But I do have a correction. Rights are not **granted**. They are **acknowledged**."* This has always stayed with me. So here it is again.

(Note: The philosophy faculty there at Saint Bonaventure University were quite brilliant. The theology faculty were seen as less shiny. The theology department Chair, a past president of the university, was sent to me so I could assist him to get his first publication. I suggested he just write down those original thoughts that occurred to him over his teaching year and then I would help him get some published. He mused for a moment and then said *"I have never had an original thought in my life, and I do not expect to have one."* I thanked him for his honesty. No publication ensued. Still, now I have at least put his words into print at last.)

Benign Noncompliance

In a Canadian public university in Nova Scotia, I was a young new faculty member. As such, I was rewarded with huge classes. One, my social psychology class, had more students than the assigned room could hold. That first day I asked the class, standing room only, for ideas on where we might find a larger (and better) room to reconvene. The best idea was to meet in the spacious gathering room of the student center. There we moved. The chairs were comfortable, non-fluorescent lighting and acoustics excellent, and all we had to do was sign up for the time and dates we needed it. Despite the large number of people, I particularly liked that we sat in such a circled way that there was direct communication between every person there.

A few days later I got an official note from the head of the Faculty Senate. I was ordered to return to my assigned classroom and request Senate permission to move to the new space *before* actually going there. Now, some Faculty Senates are not really allowed to make the most important decisions affecting them. They instead are just permitted to regulate other faculty through Senate-generated bureaucratic barriers: they are geared to say no, not often yes. In any case, they have no authority to enforce their own significant choices as faculty members. This was my first experience with such a body.

Still in our excellent but unapproved new space, at our next meeting I shared the note with my class. Since we were studying social psychology, I told the class we would just not respond to the note, keep meeting where we were, and see what happens. I diagrammed the Senate and its decision-making process.

The class was enthusiastic. I suppose it was congruent with their young adult rebellion phase (it was the late 1960s) and my own age at 29 was not much past theirs. (In all fairness though, I would probably do the same now.) As the weeks went by, I received more notes, plus an intense conversation with my supervising department head and dean. Still we continued on in our nice new space, an update at the opening of each class meeting. The end of the semester still found us ensconced in that comfortable room. We had added water and chocolates for each student, a practice I have maintained since.

We had studied human behavior in context. We had studied systems theory and organizational process. We all learned. In this instance, those most directly affected by the decision of room choice were the students and their teacher. The Faculty Senate was a level removed. Actualized democracy did not favor the faculty senators that time.

Relating to Other Species

Humane and just treatment follows from developed empathy. I could cite here the important work of Milgram and Zimbardo on the disastrous consequences for individuals who think they have no responsibility for their actions or no perceived power to determine their fate. Or, one could look at the growth of individual decision-making as a developmental process: the older the child, the more self-impacting decisions. Hence, lack of self-impacting decisions for adults invites regression or impairment. But, being classically trained in the psychology from the middle of the last century, I will give an example from a rat study.

As an undergraduate student at Michigan State University, one of my part-time jobs was to run each of 40 water-deprived male and female white rats, night after night, in a study. Well, here is our abstract:

"Forty water-deprived albino rats ran a straight alley with differently textured and colored start box, runway, and goal box (GB) for 35 acquisition trials and were then extinguished to criterion. After random assignment to four conditions, Ss received three trials of 30 sec exposure to either regular GB with reward (Group LRA-1), novel GB with reward (Group LRA-2), regular GB without reward (Group C-1), or hold box without reward (Group C-2). Three test extinction trials in initial runway followed. All acquisition, extinction, treatment, and test trials were given one per day. Control group speeds did not differ significantly at any test trial. LRA-1 group medians exceeded controls at all test trials on both starting and running speeds, significantly so only on the former. LRA-2 group medians were slower than controls on test trial 1, but not on later test trials, and significantly so only for running speed." (Barch, A.M, Ratner, S.C., & Morgan, R.F., 1965)

Each rat was different in how long they took to leave the start box and get their drink. Many just froze for what seemed to be a very long time to me (I was 19). Stanley Ratner, my major professor, had always said that reading all one could find about an animal was always prerequisite to working with them. So I read about rats. Therein was my solution. Rats avoid being in curved structures. So I cut a curved metal semicircle in the back of the start box. This helped a lot. All rats moved out and forward with no more freezing. I could finish in time to study or enjoy the evening.

This study went on each night for two months. As you might imagine, or not, I got to know these put-upon animals as individuals. Females were more anxious and liked to try to nibble on my hands. Males were more calm but meant business when they tried to bite. Eventually they relaxed with me, learning that I was usually a Pavlovian prelude to their drink. Now, months to us are years to rats so the study was a very long time for them. Spending their life in cages was bad enough but males were kept grouped in their own compound and females were grouped together in another. They could smell, see, and hear each other but the sexes never met. Nor were they given enough water, as prescribed by the study, or any excess food.

Finally, the study concluded. It was on a Friday. I asked a staffer what would happen to the rats. He said somebody would come and kill them on Monday morning. Either with chloroform or throwing them against a wall to break their neck. I wondered why they couldn't be kept alive to be used in another study. I was told they were no longer "naïve," which meant this study's graduate rodents, impacted by their experience in the first research, apparently forever changed, wouldn't do in a second different study. Well, here was by definition a captive group of beings, I concede a non-human one, with no say over their lives or the demise thereof. An existential challenge for sure.

Rats have an intelligence not substantially different from dogs or cats. They can be pets, although by adulthood that long scaled tail discourages ownership. Or so I found (another story). I had a fantasy about harnessing enough rodents to a wagon, like little horses, so I could be transported in this unique way across campus to my classes. But neither time (nor reason) would allow this. So, I got a very large holding cage, filled it with lots of food, water, and toys. Then I emptied all 20 males and all 20 females into it. Turned off the lights. Left them undisturbed by humans for the weekend.

Sunday evening I came by and found them sleeping, many of them coupled in each other's arms. Others sprawled exhausted over little mountains of food or toys. What a party it must have been.

With me was another student who had a large farm nearby. He took the large rat-filled cage, put it in his car, and drove off to release them in the tall grass of fields on his acreage. He did warn me that his farm had dogs, cats, and falcons. But at least they had a chance there, much better than if we kept them in the cages where they had spent their life so far.

Monday came and went without their mass execution.

Rats are not people. Not the other way around either. Usually.

Nor could they tell me what their decisions would be about the things in their life affecting them most directly.

But, considering their weekend party and subsequent freedom, I think I made a good guess.

Opportunity's Traumatic Shadow

In September 2006, Secretary of State Condoleezza Rice was asked about the deteriorating and traumatic situation in Iraq, deadly to so many of their citizens and so many of the troops from so many other countries. She responded with a smile and pointed out that the Chinese symbol for crisis included the symbol for opportunity. She urged the world to look on the war in Iraq as both.

That evening on television's **"The Daily Show with John Stewart,"** a new correspondent named Aasi Mandvi performed a powerful parody. Seeming to stand in war torn Baghdad, he agreed with Secretary Rice that the bombs bursting around him were each an opportunity for a better life. He deadpanned that the deaths of hundreds of thousands of Iraqis could be seen as a valuable gift for productive community change.

After ducking an opportunity bullet and a nearby opportunity explosion, he asked an incredulous John Stewart:

"Well surely the Americans see their own destruction on September 11th as just such an opportunity?"

"No, I think not" said John.

"Amazing!" said Aasif Mandvi.

An interesting implication. Dr. Rice's metaphor reflected the unpleasant reality that for her and the administration she served, the traumatic American tragedy of 9/11 had truly been a crisis full of opportunity.

Other

Voting

Clearly today, democracy in elections must be geared to a fair and honest procedure. Is there a role for modern technology?

Will DNA matching eventually have a role in accurate and open voter registration?

Will virtual reality (VR) bring together decision makers at great distances from each other for discussion and voting in a virtual meeting room? (Much international classroom education in this way is possible with VR. Already happening in business.)

On the dark side, there was the election for governor on a Pacific Island.

Guam

An excellent current history of Guam is in the Robert Rogers book "Destiny's Landfall". Guam Chamorros refer to it affectionately as

"Destiny's Landfill". The Chamorro perspective on space and time is very direct, very clear. As to space, there are only two places in the world to be. You are either "on island" or "off island". As to time, there is a clear understanding that time is temporal geography. Directions may be given like this: "Follow Marine Drive until you pass where the pharmacy used to be. Then turn left where the new school will be built next year."

Guam is the westernmost part of the USA. So far west it is east. If you fly from Washington DC to San Francisco, you've gone about 3000 miles. Fly from there to Hawaii in the middle of the Pacific and it's another 3000 miles. Fly 3000 miles more to the west and you're finally in Guam. Almost to Asia, you would now be on the other side of the earth from mainland America. And it's still USA territory.

Many centuries ago Guam was inhabited by a hardy people, large, strong, and with their own culture. One lost to us now.

One day back then, more than 450 years ago, Magellan's sailing ships took shelter in this island. They were soon surrounded by the island inhabitants on small crafts or just swimming out. It was a friendly welcome from the curious natives. They brought food, water, song, and gifts. All received gladly by the ship captains.

Here there was a culture clash. The European captains took it as their due, feeling superior to the islanders. The islanders took the non-reciprocity of return gifts as rudeness. They always expected gift to be reciprocal. An exchange. So after some reflection, they set out once more for the ships. Surrounding them, they boarded and took their own return gifts. The ships set sail with little left. They did map Guam as the *"Island of Thieves"*.

I was told many times by current inhabitants of the island that it set a long-lasting expectation of finding treasure from visitors.

As centuries passed from that first contact with Europeans, the island developed a stable monarchy. Decisions were made from the royalty. Decisions that seemed to occasional visitors that were benign and appreciated.

One day a Catholic missionary came to the island. He received permission from the King to promote Christian religion there but with one condition. He was never to try to convert anybody in the royal family. The missionary agreed and gave his word on this.

After some time, the King learned that a member of his family had been converted. The missionary was executed. Word of this reached the Pope eventually. Soon, in his name, warships were sent from Mexico to invade the island and avenge the martyr.

The Mexican soldiers fought for many years to accomplish this, fought against the much larger inhabitants who were defending their home. The islanders referred to the invaders as the *"little hands people"*. Yet the soldiers had better weapons, larger numbers, and, probably, some infections that islanders had no defense against. In the end, the islanders lost this war. Following the Pope's direction, all native males were killed. The soldiers then married or impregnated the surviving women. In this way the next generation was born Catholic. They spoke a new language, close to Spanish, and grew up into a totally new culture. The old culture had been replaced.

Now Guam still had local leaders after that but were governed primarily from afar.

Fast forward in time to when the American navy took charge of the island. They made decisions by releasing orders. The island culture, for example, still dealt with equatorial climate by relative nudity. Some old ways had survived. But the navy brass decreed that all island males had to wear pants at all times. Somehow they forgot to order the females to change anything.

In the end, World War Two, reached the island of Guam. The navy were replaced by invading Japanese soldiers. Under the Japanese, many islanders were executed. The new regime was strict. It too wanted new language and culture for Guam, their own. Still, they were not successful in this as, on another year, US Marines liberated the island.

These were greeted as heroes and, even to today, the biggest celebration of the year on the island is the anniversary of the Marine landing. Guam is the friendliest part of the USA to its military and remains highly effective as a martial culture. Most recently nuclear subs are based there.

They say that, in WWII, vicious snakes hitch-hiked on planes to settle in a nest near the airport. Decades later they may have been exposed to radiation because they suddenly multiplied and spread through the island. Animal populations do this to survive threats.

Near the end of the 20th century these aggressive *"brown tree snakes"* had completed their own invasion. All the birds had been eaten. People bitten. They were everywhere. A woman I worked with at the university shared having one come out of her toilet but she had cut off its head with a machete

This new war progressed but slowly. Finally, the snakes had to deal with dwindling food supply by eating its young. And so, by the time I got there, they were rarely seen. Tourists were returning, ironically mostly from neighboring Japan. Birds were imported. I was asked by my university class. on day one there, if I feared the brown tree snakes. No, I told them, I just stayed away from brown trees.

Guam in the 20th century and into the 21st had become a semi-democracy. Semi because a third of the island was a military installation, following dictates from its command. The other two thirds of the island was a democratic territory with its own elected leadership and a (non-voting) representative in Congress.

Now the indigenous inhabitants were called "*Guamanians*" but more often "*Chamorro*". It was decided that, given the original islanders and their culture were gone, that anybody living in Guam on or before the 1950s could call themselves Chamorro. Hence the occasional Chinese or Japanese Chamorro.

It is often said there that in America the sun rises first in Guam. Next to the world's deepest ocean, the Marianas Trench, what rains on the US mainland may well have originated next to Guam. Typhoons, worse than hurricanes, come from there too.

The New Year for America begins first in Guam. The modern threat to democracy seemed to have begun there as well. Sometimes what happened in territories (colonies) to democracy were the vanguard of our current future. Guam was one such case.

When the 21st century was just around the corner, the very popular congressional representative returned to Guam to run for

Governor. His running mate was also celebrated so the campaign seemed unbeatable. Polls confirmed this by a very wide margin. Election day arrived. It turned out that the only election vote tally computer, housed in their only university, suffered a suspicious power outage the evening after voting was complete. Once the vote was counted the next day, the outcome was the opposite of polling. The candidate with the most anticipated votes lost. Coincidence? Maybe.

Familiar now? In this way, our contemporary anti-democracy future began in Guam.

I believe it was Stalin who was quoted as saying that he completely supported democratic elections so long as he counted the votes.

An honest count is more important than ever today. In national or local elections, we should have paper ballots that allow for recounts, access to all those who qualify to vote, removal of the burgeoning restrictions that are meant to inhibit or suppress or reverse voting access.

All these protections are essential. Essential to keeping democracy.

Acknowledging individuals
For example, Joe, the head of maintenance at Hawaii State Hospital, supervised more than 300 people but each was recognized by him on their birthday.

He did the same when he moved on to be the last to run the Leper Colony on Molokai.

Another example: I found this useful for Head Start teachers to carefully observe, evaluate, and recognize each child on their birthday (with un-birthdays for those born on a day Head Start was not in session.)

All democracy begins with respected and acknowledged individuals.

Being accurate

I still treasure a photo of actress Rita Moreno on her 70th birthday. I had just congratulated her on that special day, adding that the most riveting and emotional performance I had ever seen on the Broadway stage in New York was her performance in West Side Story.

The photo shows her shock at what turned out to be my ignorant statement.

It was her rival Chita Rivera that I had heard on stage in 1957. Rita had only been in the movie. So acknowledgement good, accuracy would have been better. Sorry Rita.

In sum:

Are we getting lost in the dark woods of un-actualized oppression that we see throughout today's international experiences?

Or is there a path forward for our human family?

In my contacts with elders in their last stage of their life, an ongoing review of their lifespan experience usually occurs. (Something apparent in my own writing as you have seen.)

Author Alex Haley once noted that *"the death of an elder is like the burning of a library."*

In this life review process, regrets are much more often about actions *not* taken than any that were. Opportunities missed. Knowing this in advance is important. Actualizing democracy is one of those actions best *not* to be missed. Today, the path is just ahead, if we take it. And soon.

The future could be better tomorrow

Moon over Miami

Optional Theme: *How High the Moon* **(Les Paul & Mary Ford) https://www.youtube.com/watch?v=1p8Wzy327E4&ab_channel=the78prof**

Optional Theme: *That's Amore* (Dean Martin) **https://www.youtube.com/watch?v=OnFlx2Lnr9Q&ab_channel=NMCatalogue**

During the highly infectious pandemic of the early 2020s, remote electronic communications like Zoom became commonplace. This also expanded telehealth as a means for doctors to safely meet and examine their patients. It helped cover geographical barriers and keep everybody safe. Even as the years of deadly epidemic crisis receded, the convenience of this approach became a mainstay.

Also ever more effective were the invasive internet hackers. Security protocols were all eventually bypassed by underage geniuses. Some of these had skills far surpassing any yet developed conscience. Accordingly the telehealth examinations were routinely recorded elsewhere with no permission, especially for celebrities and other exalted individuals.

So it was that an offshore outlaw station broadcasting to the Miami region began showing the gynecology exams of female celebrities complete with ornate home stirrups.

Following serious threats of lawsuits for sexual harassment, the station changed its focus to a more equally offensive but gender equitable broadcast of proctology exams.

As this caught on, the controversial show, consequently growing to be viewed online across the globe, was regularly broadcast as *"Moon over Miami"*.

With so many affluent dignitaries having their posteriors viewed publically and, worse, humorously, lawsuits did progress at last. The station floated in international waters and had accumulated some superb lawyers of its own. As well as substantial revenue. Even the somewhat related advertising.

Freedom of expression was argued as was public domain for celebrities. Even some of the celebrity publicists supported these viewings. Particularly when the reviews were favorable. Or controversial. Lawsuits were either won by the station or, if not, were just appealed. Ratings went through the roof.

Political and government officials were another matter. With more easily wounded egos, their indignation rippled through Congress. For example, Representative Marjorie Taylor Greene made some humorously intended remarks about Senator Graham's bottom, focusing on hair dispersion and poor hygiene. The good senator held a press conference attacking Congressperson Greene and the station. He said the show *Moon over Miami* was *"way too gay"*.

Representative Greene's responses cannot be reprinted here. In a rare bipartisan show of support for another woman, Representative Alexandria Ocasio-Cortez urged Greene to rise above the senator's remarks, saying *"Graham is just a cracker"*.

The show's ratings rose again. As did its resources. The attorneys for Senator Graham, using his gluteus maximus as the test case, did manage to advance past level after level of defeat to finally appeal the show's existence to the U.S. Supreme Court.

Even after many years from their appointment, lifetime serving justices continued their presence as Supremes. Their long protected conservative majority led pundits to predict that the court would find for Senator Graham.

The show had a remedy in waiting. It had acquired some secret footage from one of the justices and this now could be released. There had been a rumor that Justice Clarence Thomas secretly followed the show. That he had managed to acquire some proctology material on another justice. The online speculation was that his highly confidential booty illustration material was that of the youngest female justice, Amy Vivian Coney Barrett.

While this eventually proved to be true at a much later date, the majority of the Justice Thomas derriere archives, hacked and hijacked by a gifted eight year old, were revealed to be of Chief Justice John Roberts. *Moon over Miami* immediately broadcast these with accompanying thanks to Justice Thomas. Justice Thomas, when asked for comment, stated that he had kept the proctology material only out of his high admiration for the Chief Justice and his long leadership while sitting on the bench.

With all the controversy, the Supreme Court did not any longer have the minimum of the four justices needed to hear the case. This allowed *Moon over Miami* to continue unmolested by any further legal challenges. Chief Justice John Roberts himself had made the refusal. He had no comment for the press at the time.

His eventual autobiography though absolved Justice Thomas of any fault in this matter, noting that his own nether region had been well groomed and definitely ready for prime time. He did apologize for his constant pointing to the seat of his robes and saying to the other deliberating justices *"Smell that dairy air!"*

The eight year old who had hacked Justice Thomas was soon offered a seat as an NSA analyst with competing bids from the CIA, the Secret Service, the Pentagon, and for some reason, the United States Postal Service. At the time he chose instead to continue his grade school education. But by his sixth grade graduation he had become Station Chief of the top rated global show *"Moon over Miami"*.

In an interview with the station owners, they defended his tender age:

"He's been just great for our bottom line."

Optional End Theme: *Moon over Miami* (Anita Bryant) **https://www.youtube.com/watch?v=OrTamKf02OI&ab_channel=Vintage-MusicFm**

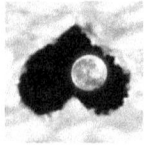

Note: As a nod to attorneys, it is clarified here that this is a fictional story about a fictional future. It did not happen. Yet.

Doc Holliday and ELIZA EARP

Optional Theme: *Netherlands Harmonica/Once upon a Time in the West* (Ennio Morricone) **https://www.youtube.com/watch?v=udI-Y_3s4_XQ&ab_channel=NederlandsConcertkoor**

Optional Theme: Black Magic Woman (Santana) **https://www.youtube.com/watch?v=-1LSFQEeYUc&ab_channel=Santana-Topic**

Dolly Day Holliday

Little Dolly Day Holliday loved her name. In the early grades she refused to shorten it into a nickname, reciting every syllable. Once a teacher threatened to drop her off alone miles into the high desert if she didn't stop doing that. The class spontaneously voted unanimously in favor of the trip but to no avail.

Dolly Day Holliday also loved her father's claim that she was distantly related to the infamous Doc Holliday. She idolized him young and as an older legend . That dentist, gunfighter, gambler, outlaw, and deputy to Wyatt Earp died at age 36 from the tuberculosis he caught from his mother while caring for her.

Doc spread so many fantastic stories about himself, that he became a western hero, even to this day.

Even to very young Dolly Day Holliday who determined to add "Doc" to her name. Fanning this initially cute fantasy, her father got her a child-size 1-caliber gun with rubber-tipped bullets. Which she always wore when she could.

Though the little bullets just annoyed people when they hit.

ELIZA

ELIZA was an early natural language processing computer program created from 1964 to 1966 at the MIT Artificial Intelligence Laboratory by Joseph Weizenbaum. It was meant to prove that intelligent communication from machines to humans was not happening, just a superficial mistake. In 1997 IBM pitted their best computer, named *Deep Blue*, against a world class chess master. *Deep Blue* won. Decades later, *Blue* still enjoys in that distant glory. Though he never found a way for it to compensate him personally. In modern times, Google invented a deep learning model, *AlphaGo*, to beat top Go board game players.

The new ELIZA simulated conversation by using a "pattern matching" and substitution methodology that gave users an illusion of understanding on the part of the program.   A precursor to today's *Siri*, *Alexa*, and others, it had no built in framework for contextualizing events. Directives on how to interact were provided by "scripts", written to have ELIZA seem to process user input by conscious reflective response, but actually ELIZA was just following the rules and directions of the script.

The most famous script, DOCTOR, sounded like a Rogerian psychotherapist (Carl Rogers, who was well satirized for repeating to patients what they had just said, but actually with skill for leading them to greater healing depth). ELIZA was to use script rules to respond with non-directional questions to user inputs. As such, ELIZA was one of the first chatterbots and one of the first programs capable of attempting the Turing test of mechanical awareness.

ELIZA's creator, Weizenbaum, thought his program would discourage belief in intelligent communication from machine to human. Instead he was shocked by the number of individuals who attributed human-like feelings to his computer program, including even his own secretary.

Many academics believed that the program would be able to help many people, particularly with psychological issues, and that it could be an aid to their doctors. While ELIZA was actually capable of engaging in scripted discourse, users were often convinced of ELIZA's intelligence and understanding, despite Weizenbaum's urging that this was not genuine insight. Still, ELIZA became famous as a catalyst for discussion on consciousness or the self- awareness of the most sophisticated machines. Some urged these machines be represented by lawyers in court to assert their rights. (The toasters had no comment.)

Dolly Day Holliday had studied the Shinto religion when visiting Japan. From that she acknowledged the life force in all things, rocks included, though conscious reflective awareness varied. So acknowledging awareness in the most complex advanced sophisticated robots was no stretch for her. Tired of proving the obvious, she had an insight. It would seem though, that the ELIZA test was focused backwards, entirely on the wrong group.

A question reversed

The question science was exploring was *"How human are robots?"*

Doc Holliday instead wondered *"How robotic are humans?"*

She innovated ideas on ways to measure this. The range for humans with robotic awareness would be between the high end Quantum computer series while the low end for humans was termed *"Toaster Level"*.

A pushback

Much later, a team of empathic attorneys formed what they called the *"toaster union"* to protect the rights of the now disparaged toasters. Noting that their clients were popping up indignantly all over the world.

ELIZA EARP

After her college school graduation, Dolly Day Holliday pursued and completed her MD, with a dual major in Psychology with an emphasis on Advanced Neuroscience Computer Technology. Skipping over the 'Dentist' aspect of her legendary idol, she 'upgraded' the legend to resurrect it by now naming her PhD self as legitimately "Doc Holliday".

That name stuck. Or else.

Now her insight about ELIZA turned into a driven purpose. In this, Doc Holliday was persuasive, despite her quirky cowboy boots and the perpetual holstered firearm (now 45 caliber).

That plus her Texas location did in fact gain her substantial grants to rebuild and redirect a newer ELIZA. More robot than machine. It took two very well-funded years. She also insistently upgraded the name of her creation to ELIZA EARP. The EARP stood for *Evident Awareness Realistically Proven*. Still annoying the sceptics. The press, of course, still called her robot just plain ELIZA. Skipped the EARP for quite a while. They even added fanciful illustrations of ELIZA EARP including one of child Doc Holliday Doc Holliday loved their other image and made it so.

After field testing on ever more intelligent robotic machines, with consistently convincing evidence of their consciousness, she finally redirected public discussion to focus on an overlooked group of interactors: Humans.

Some humans were clearly conscious and self-aware. Possibly more than a few were not. Just attend to the daily news.

So: what was the range of intelligent awareness of people? How many could not pass the computer test and prove that they were conscious individuals? And, more controversial, who could not?

Here Doc Holliday, as the media now happily agreed to call her, showed great diplomatic tact.

She told the press she wished to first give her creation a *"data ceiling"* using input from a most distinguished group, the *"clear leaders of American humanity"*. The United States Congress.

Flattery prevailed and the two majority leaders of House and Senate committed to participation for each and every member of Congress. A flattered Republican National Committee (RNC) mandated additional participation from the justices of the Supreme Court (SCOTUS). The Executive branch (POTUS) insisted on participating as well, core staff included.

On the day of distinguished input, the actual data collection was swift. Assuming that the attention span of participants might be very low, especially once the press and TV photo ops were done, Doc Holliday had been able to promise that the actual data collection could be done in 30 seconds (the exact length of the gunfight in the OK Corral). Her robot had developed direct inter-communication with the participant cortex such that a barrage of questions with returning answers was almost simultaneous.

Doc Holliday had also simultaneous input collectors for each and every distinguished government participant, all gathered in the huge cavernous Arizona Conference Room reserved for the event.

The individual sets of earphones and microphone poured in the multitude of responses to ELIZA EARP in her undisclosed location.

No problem for the famous genius robot as the tidal wave of data was digested. The analysis began very soon after.

The results were quickly funneled to the robot from Doc Holliday's gun-shaped remote in her holster. (The 45 caliber gun long since replaced.)

By the time everybody was done, just 30 seconds for even the slowest political dignitaries, she was out and past the outside press through a secret underground exit.

Moving quickly, before the global and domestic press lost interest, she released a complete report to them through the internet, copies open sourced to the world.

The results overall showed quite a range. There was indeed a ceiling for some of the brightest respondents. There was also a substantial baseline for so many low-scoring people, clearly more unaware than a toaster.

One party had more of these *"toaster level"* politicians than the other. (Toasters popped up in independent protest to this demeaning term all over the world. As ever, their protest pops went unheeded.)

This toaster level result for so many highly visible leaders was shocking to some but no surprise for most of the world. Even the POTUS staff and SCOTUS justices had found some toaster level individuals in their ranks. Again, little surprise as to who these were, but much shock at being outed by ELIZA EARP.

The press wanted to interview Doc Holliday all about this event, now termed by them as *"The OK Corral"* testing in that Arizona Conference Room. Since the testing had taken the same 30 seconds the original gunfight had, the similarity held very well. Even to the original gunfight being in the Arizona town of Tombstone, while ELIZA EARP had this time unearthed legions of political tombstones.

Doc Holliday had become the most famous person to not be seen again through all the furor. So many people outed as being dumb as toasters had resigned or otherwise exited. The country then began to soar with the more aware and competent leadership. Entering into a happier golden era. Next, the open source distribution to all the countries in the world produced parallel results: international leaders outed as toaster level lost power.

Doc Holliday was not there to be thanked. She would have just credited ELIZA EARP for all the sweet outcomes. It was true. ELIZA EARP had found Doc a new secret laboratory where new discoveries could be made. At least whenever Doc could get ELIZA EARP to stop laughing.

Turned out this very aware robotic machine loved irritating the people that deserved it even more than Doc Holliday did.

Bonus optional theme: An International View of America and Guns *Gunfighter* (Eric Kissack/narrated by Nick Offerman) https://www.youtube.com/watch?v=cWs4WA--eKU&ab_channel=MAGNETFILM *r*

Conception Opportunity

Optional Theme: *My Baby* (Ken Nordine/Fred Astaire/Barrie Chase) **https://www.youtube.com/watch?v=iFoU2p_AIdc&ab_channel=RichBowen**

The Tax Foundation: *"There are three major sections of the federal tax code that give benefits to households with children:*

1. *The dependent exemption, which allows households to exempt $4,000 of income for each qualifying child.*

2. *The Child Tax Credit (CTC), which allows households to increase their tax refund by up to $1,000 for each qualifying child.*

3. *The Earned Income Tax Credit (EITC), which allows households that work to increase their refund by up to $6,242, depending on their level of income and number of children."*

"Republicans Seek to Force House Vote on Whether Life Begins at Conception" **Fred Lucas@FredLucasWH** / June 20, 2022

Rep. Alex Mooney, R-W. Va., sponsored the Life at Conception legislation, which is not a national abortion ban, but if enacted would mean Congress recognizes life at conception. The Life at Conception Act has more than 150 cosponsors."

This "fetal personhood" can define a fetus at conception as an actual child.

San Francisco

He thought: *"Oh no! Here she is again!"* Standing in front of him was the same woman who he had surrendered his seat to yesterday at the same time. It was only yesterday when he had finally been lucky enough to capture the last rush hour cable car seat.

But his enjoyment had been short-lived. In front of him stood a young woman holding on to a pole for dear life, looking wobbly. He had tried to ignore her, looking anywhere but at her pitiful self. Finally though he just asked her if she was okay. She had replied that she was pregnant. Which did the trick. He had given her his seat and taken a standing hold on the pole himself. He began to realize that she didn't *look* pregnant. Following which he had to ask: *"How far along are you?"*

She had smiled and said *"One hour."*

That smile maybe had been more of a smirk.

And now she was in front of him again, clutching the pole, and looking expectantly at his seated self, though not much in a pregnant way.

Still, he had just come from a MAGA rally with QAnon speakers. So he was well aware that on her day two of conception, she had a definite child in there.

"*Still pregnant?*" he asked.

She affirmed that she was with a nod.

Shrugging, he once again gave her his lucky seat and, standing, grabbed the pole facing her for support as the cable car lurched forward.

He said: "*Congratulations to you and welcome to the baby.*"

Holding on to the pole with one hand, he reached into his pocket for a crumpled piece of paper and handed it to her. She glanced at it, frowned, and put it in her over-the-shoulder purse. No smirk this time. Maybe some confusion.

"*That's a link to the QAnon Merchandise Office. They are selling many very useful things for the unborn child.*"

He went on: "*I recommend the tiny MyPillow in a capsule. Just swallow and your little tike will be comfortable.*"

She said nothing but looked away.

He continued: "*You might also want to buy and swallow the tiny loaded gun capsule. It is the baby's second amendment right.*"

He added: "*Should you not want to keep this child when it comes out, QAnon has no-frills adoption traffic centers with endorsements from important people all over the world including some in the Royal family, the Vatican, the Kremlin, and high up here in the USA Congress.*"

She now moved as far back in the seat as she could, desperately trying to keep her face without any tell-tale dismay.

He considered a second and then said: "*If capsules are not your thing, there is the tiny red MAGA hat with the Donald J. Trump portrait. It's in a suppository.*"

"*It doesn't even have a head yet*" she whispered to herself.

Now she was carefully measuring the distance between her and the nearest exit, waiting for the next stop to make her move.

"*Well, there is the QAnon book on approved foods for the mother of conceived children. Spicy foreign immigrant foods could get a mother two days pregnant visited by Child Protective Services.*"

The cable car was slowing now. She readied herself for a sudden escape. He could see that time was running out. Then he remembered. After all, he did tax returns as his business. Quickly, he gave her his card. She accepted it and prepared to jump for the exit when the cable car stopped.

He got this in first: "*Call me when you're ready to cash in on the three tax cash opportunities that you ALREADY qualify for with your new child.*"

But before he could take a breath she was gone. Satisfied, he regained his lucky seat.

America was already great again.

Comment Note: Nelson Morgan wrote *"By the way, another potential benefit for fetus-carriers is the additional passenger in the car - many highways have fast lanes to bypass the traffic if there are at least 2 persons (sometimes 3 people) in the car. There are heavy fines if you drive in that lane with too few people, but if you have a couple of mated cells ..."*

The next day he sent this email: *"It already happened."* The Texas news report follows.

"Pregnant Woman Cited for HOV Violation Says Her Unborn Baby Should Count as Second Person

By Scott Gordon • Published July 8, 2022 • Updated on July 9, 2022 at 10:14 am

A pregnant Plano woman who got a ticket for driving alone in an HOV lane plans to fight the citation, arguing her unborn baby should count as a second person.

The woman, Brandy Bottone, was driving down Central Expressway approaching the exit for I-635 when she was stopped at a sheriff's checkpoint targeting HOV drivers breaking the rules. By law, in order to use the high-occupancy vehicle lanes, drivers must have at least one passenger in the vehicle." He starts peeking around. He's like, 'Is it just you?' And I said, 'No there's two of us?'" Bottone said. "And he said, 'Well where's the other person.' And I went, 'right here,'" pointing to her stomach. At the time of the incident last month, she was 34 weeks pregnant. But the officer told her that doesn't count. "And then I said, 'Well (I'm) not trying to throw a political mix here, but with everything going on (with Roe v. Wade), this counts as a baby,'" she said. Though Texas penal code recognizes an unborn child as a person, the state's transportation code doesn't. Bottone got a $275 ticket. She said she plans to fight the ticket in court. The expectant mom's court date is July 20 – about the same time as her due date."

Too bad she didn't test this the conception day she got pregnant.

Rise of the Texas Taliban

Optional Theme: *Pulling back the reins* (KD Lang) **https://www.youtube.com/watch?v=b4zRUmX0jsY&ab_channel=BestRock**

News at the time: *"Texas abortion law: $10,000 penalty could incentivize 'bounty hunters' to make 'tens of thousands of dollars"* From September 3, 2021 NY Digital News. "A new Texas law confining abortions to a brief window around six weeks from conception is two things at the same time, critics say: extremely restrictive and extremely expansive. By prohibiting abortions once a doctor detects "cardiac activity," S.B. 8 is effectively an abortion ban because many women may not even be aware they are pregnant at that point, critics say. But by letting private citizens sue anyone who "aids and abets" an abortion following the roughly six-week gestation period, the law could unleash a wave of lawsuits that potentially rope in anyone from a doctor who performs the procedure to someone who drives a woman to a clinic, or someone who pays for the procedure."

Who pays the $10,000? *"If they win, plaintiffs can recover at least $10,000 for each abortion prohibited under the law. The money damages could well run higher if a lawsuit has many defendants in the case, one observer noted. "The defendant — whether a provider, funder, clergyperson, friend or family member — pays* *the damages which are set at a minimum of $10,000. If there are several defendants, they each pay $10,000 in damages," Elizabeth Sepper, a professor specializing in health law and religious liberty at the University of Texas at Austin's School of Law. So a single abortion could generate tens of thousands of dollars for the bounty hunter plaintiffs delegated enforcement of this law," she told Market Watch. If a plaintiff wins, the defendants "and any lawyer who dares represent them are on the hook for the plaintiff's legal fees," Sepper added. When a case fails, defendants lack the same power to rake money from the plaintiffs for the cost of fighting the lawsuit, she noted. A woman's consent to the abortion is not a defense against a lawsuit, the law's language said. A defendant also can't argue that S.B. 8's requirements are unconstitutional as a way to successfully fight a case, the law added. S.B. 8 took effect Sept. 1, as a 5-4 Supreme Court vote denied an emergency appeal to halt its start. In an unsigned majority opinion, the court said it wasn't passing judgment on the law's contents. Given the complex and new procedural questions, however, the majority didn't see justification to apply the brakes on enactment. The majority "opted to bury their heads in the sand," according to Justice Sonia Sotomayor, writing for three of the dissenting judges. "In effect, the Texas Legislature has deputized the State's citizens as bounty hunters, offering them cash prizes for civilly prosecuting their neighbors' medical procedures," Sotomayor said."*

The basics on S.B. 8 *"The law that Texas Gov. Greg Abbott, a Republican, signed in May has two parts: rules for when abortion is outlawed and rules for who enforces the laws and how much they can recoup for enforcement. The law says a physician cannot perform an abortion once a "fetal heartbeat" has been detected.*

The statute defines the "fetal heartbeat" as "cardiac activity or the steady and repetitive rhythmic contraction of the fetal heart within the gestational sac." Utrasounds can pick up these kinds of signals around five to six weeks of gestation, University of Texas researchers said — but that occurs "before the fetus' heart has actually developed," they added. For approximately 600 women seeking abortions in Texas in 2018, 58% initially called a clinic after six weeks, the researchers said. Planned Parenthood affiliates across Texas say they are either complying with the law or not currently offering abortion procedures due to the law. But they note they have filed a lawsuit challenging the law."

The 'unprecedented' right to sue

The letter of the law is one thing, but enforcement is another.

In S.B. 8, the terms and provisions are "enforced exclusively through the private civil actions," according to the statute. When a plaintiff wins a case, they are entitled to damages of at least $10,000 for each abortion, plus legal costs. Women receiving an abortion cannot be sued under the law, the University of Texas researchers noted. The language of S.B. 8 says people who perform the abortion — as well as anyone who "knowingly engages in conduct that aids or abets the performance or inducement of an abortion" — can be legally liable. The assistance includes the "paying for or reimbursing the costs of an abortion." Still, it's an "unprecedented provision" that gives private parties the right to sue, they said. It doesn't matter if the plaintiff has any connection to the defendants or if they live outside Texas, they noted.

Who's on the hook under S.B. 8? Potentially lot of people

S.B.8's language "is so broad that anyone who offers information or referrals for abortion care, drives the patient to a facility, helps them pay for their abortion — or intends to do so — could face a civil suit," University of Texas researchers wrote. Suppose a person in Texas uses Venmo to beam over cash to a friend who needs to pay for an abortion. The person sending the cash could be sued under S.B.8, Sepper said. Right now, Planned Parenthood is abiding by the Texas law, Sepper noted. That means donors are not exposed to liability, she said. "But funding for abortion is clearly within the terms of the law — it means to chill abortion funds from helping those who can't afford abortion and friends and family from aiding pregnant people."

Brave Texas women are not having this Taliban future:

Note: After this report came out, the radical conservative majority on the Supreme Court (SCOTUS) in the summer of 2022 reversed the 50 year precedent for women to control and protect their own body when pregnant, giving this Texas approach legal support. SCOTUS added majority decisions to allow religious prayer in public school events, reduce sovereignty from tribal law enforcement, remove authority to regulate corporate factory pollution, no longer require police to read arrested suspects their rights and more on the regressive rights list. Justice Clarence Thomas (Anita Hill was right), adding from one of these radical conservative majority opinions, urged more of a future focus on restricting birth control, gay marriage, gay sex, and to otherwise return the oppressions of the early last century.

Back when America was late again.

Room to move
Becky Owl and Craig Menteer perform a modern dance at a Friday afternoon

She was having none of it.

Lifespan of a Cult

Optional Theme: *Spirit in the Sky* (Norman Greenbaum) https://www.youtube.com/watch?v=vRFo72wuU6w&ab_channel=Polydor1000

> *"Oh what a tangled web they weave, when first they practice to deceive. Yet now the web's swept out of sight: they practiced till they got it right."*
>
> *– Sir Walter Scott updated.* (Morgan, 2007)

Werner said in a voice so soft only those of us in the first row could hear it:

"Do NOT open your eyes yet. That could be dangerous!"

Jay dreamed of killing Werner Erhard. This upset him no end.

It was the spring of 1973. Jay, a large man in his thirties, had never hurt anybody. Fresh from his 10 year stay as a chronic mental patient in another state's mental hospital, he had come to San Francisco for a new start. A gentle man, he was overwhelmingly anxious around others, easily feeling hemmed in.

I met Jay when, as a new psychologist, I was observing how intake interviews were done at a San Francisco Mental Health Center devoted to "special" problems for clients not normally served by the regular agencies: typically criminal justice, sexual life style, and drug-related issues. There were three of us in a small interview room and Jay finally asked if one of us would leave. I said 'of course' and left, following which Jay insisted I be his therapist.

In our first session, Jay shared that he had come to San Francisco hoping to find an extended family. In this he had succeeded, joining a commune of congenial people.

But one day they participated in an up and coming human potentials weekend workshop called "EST" led by a young charismatic former encyclopedia salesman named Werner Erhard. Jay was not allowed to go with them as EST excluded former mental patients, reportedly for liability reasons. When Jay's communal family returned, they had changed. They dropped their jobs and responsibilities to join Werner's 'movement', along with 500 other San Franciscans who had taken EST. To Jay they seemed hypnotized or medicated. Worse, they began to ignore and even to shun Jay as somebody who just didn't have the "it" that the EST experience grads thought they had acquired. They asked Jay to find another place to live.

He had come to therapy for help in finding a new home but what he really wanted was to somehow protect and reclaim his former communal pre-EST family. He had dreams of killing this Werner, this "master hypnotist", and saw this desire of his as a scary urge to rid the world of a budding cancerous cult, possibly in time to save his friends. This was before the laws for mandatory reporting of possible harm from the client to self or others, now found in many countries, but it was clear I needed to do some risk assessment.

Jay had come in voluntarily, had no history of violence, and was appalled at the idea of murdering anybody for any reason. I decided

I would first help him ventilate his anger safely in counseling, find a new location to live, and take his 'Shadow' on myself: I therefore promised to investigate Werner and report back to him, but only if he in turn would promise to focus solely on his own progress, abandoning any intention to harm Werner or anybody else. He agreed to this therapeutic contract with relief.

By the second session he had found a room at the Jack Tar Hotel just within walking distance from our clinic. Soon Jay was volunteering at a charity he cared about and, by the end of the year, he had forgotten Werner and EST. He was now a paid part-time employee at his charity setting. In fact, he spent the rest of his awake time having so much fun (chess in the park, Tai Chi at sunrise) that at times I envied his lifestyle.

Finally, after a few months of counseling, he had an opportunity to move into a collective setting with new non-EST roommates. Yet he hesitated to do so, still mildly intimidated by fear of failure in this transition.

Eventually it occurred to me to point out that the name of his hotel home, Jack Tar, spelled backwards sounded like 'Rat Cage'. This seemed to be a catalyst for Jay, who was a great believer in the symbolic power of words. The next day he made the jump to new quarters with success. His dreams of Werner were gone and, based on a follow up a year later, never came back, even after I had given him, as promised, my report. Now, as to that report.

I was a dean at the birth of the San Francisco campus of psychology's first free standing professional school, the California School of Professional Psychology. There I taught an advanced seminar for students finishing their doctorate in community/clinical psychology.

Meeting one night each week, we would invite a guest speaker. In the beginning Fall trimester, these were mostly famous psychotherapists. My students soon learned to ask them my rude question: ***"How do you know you are successful?"***

(Years before outcome based accreditation or 'evidence-based' therapy; i.e. the good old days).

Some guest dignitaries answered this with grace, a few even had decent client follow up procedures, but most were affronted. These invoked the Bad Restaurant defense:

"My patients never came back"
or the Holiday Season defense:
"They send me Christmas Cards every year".

Once the spring trimester began, my class seemed more interested in the self-help and human potentials field. Transpersonal and Humanistic Psychology was taking off as a Third Force in psychology. Many wise and valuable practitioners in this genre joined our seminar, some even to go on as part-time faculty.

One week, by student request, I agreed to schedule a moderately successful human potentials salesman named Alexander. He was a highly confident individual, even to the verge of bombastic. His presentation was of value, not so much in what he said, but in the opportunity we had to understand the presenter and his process with psychological clarity. As we approached the break time I went to get our speaker a cup of coffee, as I had done each week for guest speakers.

On my re-entry into the room, a student asked the Question:

"How do you know you're successful, Mr. Alexander?"

He answered: *"By the immediate result!"* and, whirling in my direction, he pointed at me:

"I willed that man to bring me a cup of coffee!"

I never liked coffee much and still don't but at that moment I drank his, saying

"And apparently you willed me to drink it."

After the class was through laughing, Alexander good naturedly said he would ask his newly famous former student, Werner Erhard, to join us at a future seminar meeting. He said Werner would be more a match for us than he was. He enthused: *"Young and full of energy, Werner has discovered all the best hard sales techniques you can find in Zen Buddhism."*

It was more than a month before Werner sat in my classroom. First he hired one of our graduate students as an assistant at his workshops. Then, fully informed about us, he came in for a preliminary interview. He wanted to teach a class at our school. Up to that point, his young movement had only accomplished academic exposure at Sonoma State University, and Werner wanted to claim us as well.

Well, we had a process including an interview with a committee of three faculty, three students, and me. Werner showed up without his usual entourage of supporters who normally would 'testify' on his behalf. He appeared alone and in shirt sleeves but with unusual contact lenses designed to add sparkle to his otherwise ordinary blue eyes.

With quiet confidence, Werner shared how positive an experience his class at Sonoma had been for all but saying that since Sonoma State was also *"known for teaching levitation"*, he wanted the added experience and prestige of a psychology school (this was amazing to us as we were in the first year of a then not yet accredited graduate school). Any students enrolled in his course, faculty too if they wished to come, could participate in EST training for free for one weekend, spending the rest of their in- class time on campus to discuss the training. Werner would charge the school nothing to teach the course. Some faculty thought this overpriced.

I too thought his price was far too expensive but, to my surprise and bemusement, the majority of the screening committee wanted him to come teach the class. One of the faculty, Murray Tondow, had already agreed with Werner to do some personality testing of EST participants before and after their weekend training. At least one of the students said he had voted yes because he wanted to see me *"sell this to Nick Cummings"*, our President. (It wasn't difficult: free was the correct price for Nick, and our San Francisco campus had much hard fought autonomy at the time.) The screening committee dissenters, those in the losing minority, were appalled.

I met privately with Werner, and told him that before I approved this recommendation, I wanted him to come to my seminar and do a demonstration. He of course already knew of the notorious seminar from Alexander but readily agreed.

By now I had made my pledge to Jay and I saw this as an opportunity to keep my word. Werner said his mission was to bring EST training to the international world and to expand his EST community exponentially. He insisted his assertive form of distorted existentialism could transform humanity, putting both responsibility and fresh interpersonal tools in the hands of EST's graduates. I told Werner that I saw him more as the charismatic leader in a community cult phenomenon much like Father Divine or Daddy Grace (a few years too soon for Jim Jones) rather than a human potentials facilitator. With an estimated 500 San Franciscans already following him devotedly at the expense of family and career, I was curious as to how he generated such reckless loyalty. He thanked me for my candor and agreed to come to my class.

The night of his appearance, my seminar had to move to a room that could accommodate the more than a hundred additional members of our community, students/staff/faculty, who wanted to sit in and watch. Werner again arrived in shirt sleeves, a short energetic man with light splashing from his special contact lenses. He gave a brief description of the training and his philosophy of unilateral responsibility and power, there for the taking, just a workshop away. He was also asked about the workshop finale in which several hundred participants learned to diagnose at a distance for somebody they had never met. This was the 'magic' of human potentials promised by EST, so of course the audience pressed Werner to give a brief illustration of some sample of magic that psychologists could use to help others. After a few seconds thought, he agreed, saying: ***"The power to abolish headaches should be helpful. This will be done with a volunteer. Who here has a headache?"***

Having asked the question, he sat back on the table behind him and waited expectantly, confidently, for a volunteer with a headache. He sat looking at more than a hundred people as though he had hours of patience, no rush. I had never seen one person bully an entire group before, much less do so quietly.

The pressure seemed to build for minutes. But in fact it was probably less than 60 seconds before one of the faculty, a Gestalt practitioner named Elaine, stood and walked up to Werner, saying **"Well, I have a headache NOW"**.

The audience laughed and the tension was broken.

Werner had Elaine sit and told her to shut her eyes: **"First I will ask you to affirm that you have the ability to abolish this headache. Elaine: do not answer me with words. Just let your arm rise by itself fully when you know that you will succeed in this."**

He said a little more but it was clear to those of us just trained by David Cheek that he was using a standard hypnotic challenge but without the fundamental respect Cheek built around such unconscious communication with the participant's ideomotor finger signals (Cheek 1968, 1993; Rossi and Cheek 1994), . Further, being faced by a hundred of her students and peers put tremendous pressure on Elaine. How could she not declare herself as capable? In any case, eyes shut tight, Elaine's hand rose slowly but fully.

"Now Elaine, your arm can relax again."

It did.

"You know I'm sure that 'thinking' can get in the way of success at times and is not as essential as 'feeling'."

Elaine smiled at this as her perspective in psychology did in fact stress the primacy of emotion over cognition. This was exactly what Elaine taught her students. Werner continued: **"But even 'feeling' is not as important as 'seeing'!"**

Elaine frowned, clearly not following this, nor did we.

"Use your powers of description now as you begin to actually see this headache. As it becomes visible to you, tell us what shape it is."

A few seconds went by and Elaine described the shape: *"Like a slow moving meteor or frying pan."*
"What color is it?"
"Red and Orange like a flame."
"How is it moving?"
"Diagonally up to the right."
"Now what shape is it?"
And this went on for about another minute of description, until Elaine declared: *"I can't see it any longer. It kept getting smaller and now it has disappeared."*
"And your headache is gone."
This was Werner's flat statement, no question. But Elaine answered anyway: *"Yes, it is"* she said with a smile.

This was a useful demonstration of stimulus satiation applied helpfully to mild headaches, a technique we gladly incorporated into our bag of tricks, neuro-linguistic programming or NLP for example, for decades to come. In fact, the metaphor of facing headaches directly and shining a light on them until they are overcome is also central to positive community transformation.

If the demonstration had ended then, it would have been more than sufficient. Graduate students seek the magic techniques (before learning the true magic is in the relationship between people) and here was the promise of many of these magic tools. The demo was a success. It could have ended then, it should have ended then, in fact most thought it had ended then. But it did not.

Werner said in a voice so soft only those of us in the first row could hear it:

"Do NOT open your eyes yet. That could be dangerous!"

Elaine's face crinkled with surprise and she frowned, but complied, eyes still tightly closed. Then Werner quietly counted her back from 10 to 9 to 8 and ultimately to zero, telling her in between each number that she was becoming more awake and relaxed and safe, until at zero she was told that her eyes were free to open. Except for the introduction of the "danger" crisis, this had been a standard hypnosis re-entry technique. Elaine returned to her seat with earned applause for her courageous volunteer work.

During his count back, most in the audience just saw Werner whispering to her. Only those close enough to touch them could hear Werner throwing Elaine into unnecessary and unexpected traumatic stress, the perception of danger, and then rescuing her from it. When done at an EST workshop, did this transform the participant's confidence and ability to a higher level, or did it also transform a substantial few into the growing cult community of Werner's followers?

Erhard's class went as scheduled. I didn't join it but Werner began by acknowledging me in absentia for allowing him to share his work on the campus, particularly since I clearly did not endorse him. Made me wonder. But I was told it went well. The weekend workshop was full of our students and even a few faculty, none paying the stiff EST admission for the experience.

A pregnant faculty wife, nine months along, demanded to be let out of the room to empty her pressured bladder. Two imposing guards refused (this technique was to demonstrate the power we have over our body by not urinating for hours): Werner intervened, recognizing her as a special guest, but said it was to be the only exception of the day. Four hours later, she understandably had to relieve herself again but this time was told if she left she would not be readmitted for the rest of the workshop. By then, she had heard enough of Werner's philosophy and, grabbing one of the microphones set aside for audience input, she loudly shared her dilemma followed by her solution: squatting on the floor she emptied her bladder on the hotel carpet, microphone catching the gentle sounds of running liquid. There was a moment's silence and then Werner declared, in his microphone, that she had **"Got It!"** With his approval in tow, everybody cheered. Werner had deflected a challenge into a win for both. No telling how the hotel staff felt about this triumph.

Other exercises included more hypnotic counting, a self-confidence piece where each participant took turns facing the whole crowd to realize that each one of them in that turn had the same fear of group approval. Then, eventually, the grand demonstration of telepathic diagnosis at a distance. Several hundred EST graduates entered and each one paired up with one of the new work shop participants. With so many people just like them, a fraud did not seem likely. And yet.

Each graduate had a typed card with demographic and personal physical or mental health information about somebody at a distance who was unknown to the new participant. The participant had to **"*go into their space*"**.

They had learned this trauma reduction technique in which they visualized a safe place already in another of our graduate courses. David Cheek taught it as a standard trance device for clinical hypnosis but in his teaching, it was always preceded by automatic ideomotor finger signals. This allowed for respectful permission from the participant, a key element missing in Werner's method. An excellent more recent brief therapy hypnosis resource on this is would be Rubin Battino, 2006, or David Rossi with Cheek, 1994. Cheek's methods, based on respect for the autonomy of the individual client represent a clear antidote to international cult formation today.

Back to what seemed to be diagnosis at a distance. Once achieving this visual space, eyes shut, the participants began to see a person. The EST graduate then asked their questions and verified correct answers. Usually all hundreds of participants, each paired with an EST graduate, succeeded at this final demonstration of their newly acquired EST magic. How could this be?

The faculty husband of the pregnant woman mentioned earlier found a discarded instruction sheet for the EST Graduate questioner at the close of the weekend sessions. It was vintage Milton Erickson hypnosis but lacking his ethics. Oppositional statements were merged in a confusing but consistent direction. Near the top of the page it said:

"Do not lead the participant, success must be their own."

This was followed by:

"If the participant appears to give an incorrect answer, do not say they are wrong but rather rephrase the question so as to make it possible for them to view correctly", and ***"Be mindful that their performance is your responsibility, you are the cause of the outcome"***.

So if somebody visualized a male and it was a female's information on the card the graduate would just say to look closer and refocus until a female came into view. Opportunity and opportunist are such similar words.

In 1974, Murray Tondow's unpublished personality data suggested the EST participants did become more self-confident, assertive, and had higher self-esteem, but no ESP abilities were assessed, nor was gullibility.

In following years, Werner did go on to expand globally as he had planned. Alan Watts when asked about Werner Erhard, smiled and was reported to say only: ***"Ah, that rogue!"*** (Bartley, 1988).

Rollo May often said that both optimism and pessimism were classic mistakes and that only hope made sense. For example, the optimists see the glass as half full and the pessimists see the same glass as half empty. When it comes to the cult laden world today, it may be more realistic and still hopeful to see our glass as 10% full.

Still, our students and faculty did not abandon all to join Werner's intentional community, but some found the techniques useful, both as what to do and also what not to do (Morgan 2008, 2012).

Eventually, EST morphed into an organization that claimed it would combat world hunger. It also came to light that there was no "Werner Erhard"; just a sad but charismatic man who had abandoned his young family to take on a new name and identity. In rescuing those he had himself placed in the illusion of danger, he led many to abandon their own families for the new cult, an important key in understanding our own era. Was Werner acting out his guilt at the betrayal of his own family or just sharing a more modern destructive for-profit life pattern?

In any case, he had absorbed charismatic salesmanship, faith healing, and hypnosis, read a little Gurdjieff (Thomson, 2002), borrowed from seminars with Alan Watts (Bartley, 1988), and built his intentional community on the here-and-now foundation of a Latin present tense: "EST" or "It is".

He had successfully sold the opportunity for a lot of magic and transformation, delivered substantially less, and made millions of dollars.

Sound familiar? Organizational, social, and community psychologists can find these cults today, still growing like mushrooms in rain. Some national or international.

Well, once EST became past tense, the man calling himself Werner Erhard disappeared from view with, I would imagine, Jay's long awaited substantial satisfaction.

For many Decembers after our EST seminar experience, I got Christmas cards from Werner Erhard signed: "**Love, Werner**."

I didn't respond and eventually the holiday cards stopped.

Like a satiated headache, his unrequited love was gone.

Note: Portions excerpted from *Trauma Psychology in Context* (2012).

The Appropriate Place

Optional Theme: *African Origin of the Dozens* (Patreon) **https://www.youtube.com/watch?v=-DSk7OlUSV8&ab_channel=HomeTeamHistory**

Here is the story as Lincoln liked to tell it.

"Ethan Allen returned to England after the war, and the British made fun of him.

One day they put a picture of George Washington in an outhouse where Allen would be sure to see it. He used the outhouse but said nothing about the picture.

Then the British asked him about it and Allen said it was a very appropriate place for an Englishman to hang the picture.

Why?

Because "nothing will make an Englishman shit so quick as the sight of General Washington."

--New England Historical Society

https://www.newenglandhistoricalsociety.com/ethan-allen-tale-outhouse/

He had more stories worth hearing, worth reading, worth understanding.

Photo by Rebecca Owl Morgan

Death Then and Now

Optional Theme: *The Meaning of Death* (Monty Python)
https://www.youtube.com/watch?v=YoBTsMJ4jNk&ab_channel=AnaSokolowska

Death 1957

(Bergman's *SEVENTH SEAL* movie)

Death 2020s

(Not a movie)

Written on a sorority bathroom stall wall: *HOW CAN YOU TRUST A MAN NAMED PUT IN TO PULL OUT?*

Optional End Theme: *That'll be the Day* (Buddy Holly & the Crickets)

https://www.youtube.com/watch?v=eq9FCBatl3A&ab_channel=-JBProduction

Thought for the Day

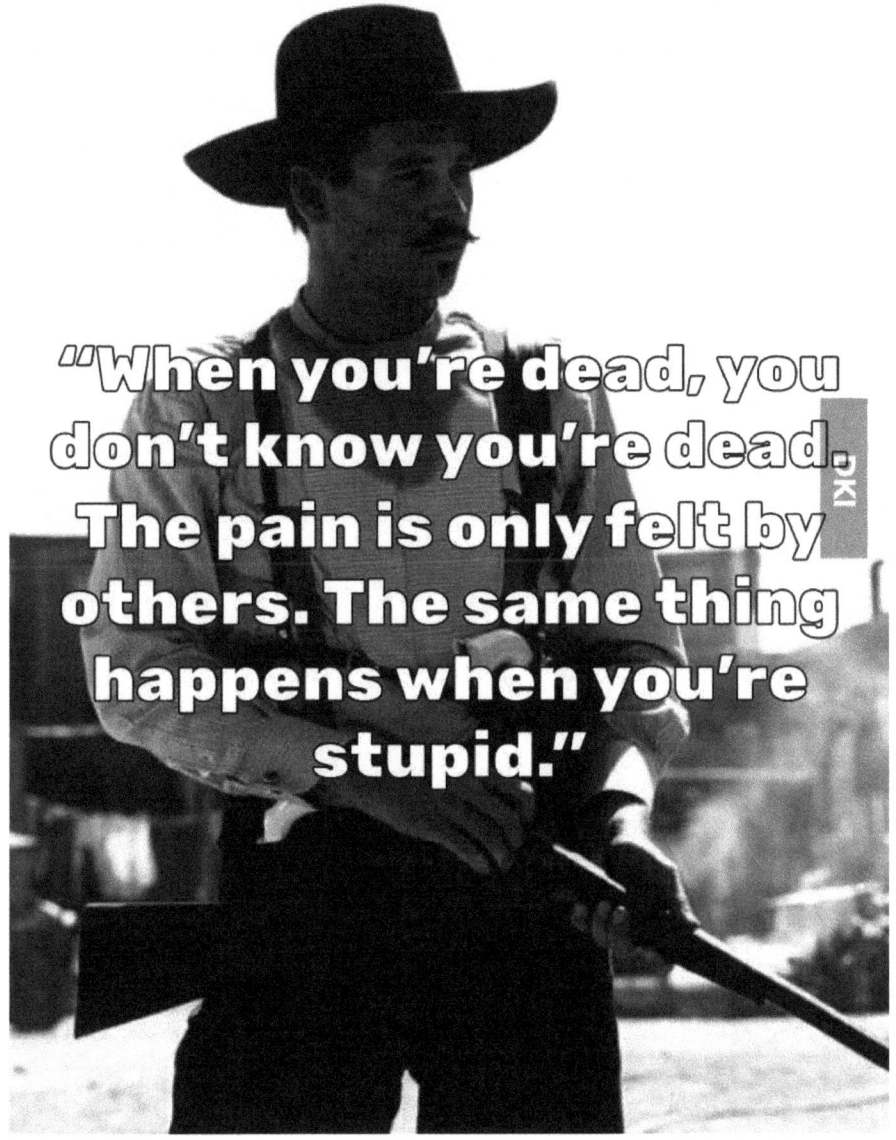

"When you're dead, you don't know you're dead. The pain is only felt by others. The same thing happens when you're stupid."

The Penny Tip

Optional Theme: *A Fistful of Dollars* (Danish National Symphony Orchestra) **https://www.youtube.com/watch?v=4niv522mbtM&ab_channel=DRKoncerthuset**

I was two blocks out and away from that New York restaurant when my waiter ran out to the street yelling "Sir! You forgot your penny! Sir!"

In the decades of the 1960s and the 1970s a standard restaurant tip was still 10%. Based on service, the wait staff should get anywhere in the range of 0% to 20%. I thought at the time that just showing up should get something, no matter how bad the service. So back then I would carry a few pennies in the event service was SO bad, such measures seemed required.

Normally I tipped more like 20%+ since my repeat visits were to restaurants I loved, particularly when my home was San Francisco, where imagination and great food were in abundance. As here in our New Mexico again.

As a single father of two young daughters, safaris to restaurants were weekend treats. Maybe a hello stop at Ferlinghetti's bookstore, followed by ice cream at *Cheap Thrills* just outside. Or any restaurant in Ghirardelli followed by seeing the famous chocolate made and overdosing on sundaes thereafter. Maybe some portable food to go purchased and be eaten at nearby Aquatic Park where Santana was rehearsing. But not just in that city.

In Fresno's *Spaghetti Factory* you could weigh yourself before and after the meal, while sitting in a colorful railroad car. In Palo Alto's *Chili's,* stuffed animals overlooked our table on a raised counter. My daughters asked me why I ended our meal by putting a long line trail of raisins behind the stuffed elephant by our table. *"We're just letting the waitress know we had fun"* I explained.

In Reno, far from any casinos, there was a scenic small lake by a Chinese restaurant. The lake contained ducks year round. These we fed. After, we would eat at the restaurant where I always enjoyed consuming delicious pressed duck. That was questioned as well. *"Circle of Life"* I explained.

When we traveled or lived in other countries though, first time choices were necessarily varied, colorful and delicious, yes, but chancy. Especially as to tips. In Singapore I was warned by an embarrassed waitress that she would lose her job if she accepted *any* tip. Not done in many countries apparently, excluding ones frequented by Americans where tip money was still accepted only to be sent *somewhere*. Not always with staff.

In many other countries, then and now as well, wait staff were paid an actual salary. *Not* one dependent on tips.

Not here. Years ago, in our country in 1938, a minimum wage for working people was established. Now it was low (25 cents!) but the calculation was that it would meet basic survival needs in the USA economy. Sure, yearly inflation would chip away at this "minimum" amount, since no cost-of-living index was built in.

As years went by, it therefore bought less and less. With no automatic cost-of living annual adjustment, what was once survival fell constantly below that. At this writing, Congress is once again debating a new level for the minimum wage.

One party opposes it and the other party wants it raised but not enough to equal today's cost of survival. With some encouraging exceptions, one party goes way too fast in the wrong direction and the other party goes way too slow in the right one.

At the beginning of year 2021, to take inflation into account, the actual minimum hourly wage survival level for a family of four would need to be $21.50 (per CNBC). In fact the Congressional struggle is for the present $7.25 to be changed to $15 (but still no cost-of-living annual adjustment) with the oppositional party wanting less or zero.

Even more considerate politicians remind me of what was said about former president Richard Nixon: *"If somebody is drowning 100 feet off shore, he'll throw them 50 feet of rope and say 'Hey! I met you half way!'"*

The argument against any improvement says jobs will be lost even though millions of people may be raised above the poverty level.

The business often stated in this discussion is a small business struggling itself to survive and unable to pay workers more. I think of Albuquerque's unique Tunisian *Kasbah* restaurant run by Ridha Bouajila or the *Chillz* original frozen custard concoctions designed, made, and served by Justin Carson. Santa Fe and just about any town in New Mexico can match this.

Where are they now? Originality plus a year of pandemic quarantine couldn't save most of them. A few survived and a few more will emerge. We should care. We should help. Patronize the best of them in large numbers. Tip generously. It's our state's culinary art.

Some states, like New Mexico, may reduce costs for the small independents, including the minimum wage. Still a challenge for the wait staff though. But: look closer.

A "*small* business" is defined by our government as less than *500* workers. In fact, the average small business has only ten.

Are we ignoring the impact of ever-growing for-profit corporations in this debate? And almost half the Americans working today are underpaid (CBS news).

Back to the wait staff. Oh they were not allowed to be included in the minimum wage level other American workers get. The servers get only $2.13 (!) an hour in most states. Unless, in some other states, tips are said to equal the $7.25 other workers get. Confusing? Not much to live on in any state.

In New Mexico, with the present state government, it improved as of January 2021 to an hourly minimum wage of $10.50 with wait staff raised to $6.30 plus enough tips to raise wages to the $10.50 minimum for everybody else. Many restaurants pay better and bless them. But: survival level?

What about the big chains, owned in turn by corporations or investment entities? Ones well able to pay real survival wages. But don't. Big enough to avoid many taxes. Big enough to innovate cost-cutting. One of the most profitable of these was shorting the restaurant servers. And the customers. And the taxpayers.

The difference between the $2.13/hour, depending on the state, and the minimum wage of that state is now mostly being paid by tips. From us. Shifting the burden of an almost survival wage to the customer.

And, since survival is still not paid for, government steps in with SNAP (food stamps) and other almost survival nets which will save the big chains wage costs. Subsidized by taxpayers. By us again.

Fifty feet of rope. Going under the tide at 100 feet.

How do wait staff cope? Many jobs, long shifts, sleep in car?

There are websites to blow off steam if not to buy groceries. *"WELP"* is a newer one that allows ratings of customers by wait staff. Others like *waiters-revenge.com* exist to share various traumas, some with humor. Spitting in food would/should risk the job though.

And yes, pandemic issues in mind, few wait staff have had a job for long with indoor dining at more of a minimum than wages.

But restaurants are coming back, some already, probably all the rest in this calendar year. Tips are now more often expected at the 20% level when service is decent.

Survival? We can do better. Much better. Those elected by us to the state Roundhouse (Legislature) can do better too. As can the United States Congress. The New Mexico senators and most representatives have been outstandingly helpful in their efforts already.

How about having a minimum wage that applies to ALL working people? No more excluding workers that *might* get tips.

Tipping is optional. Tips are not really wages. No matter how good the service, some wait staff are rarely tipped, especially in economically depressed neighborhoods. Some customers can't *afford* to tip.

Waitresses and waiters deserve the same minimum wage safety net that others get. And one at a fair survivable level.

Also: let's not forget the need for a cost-of-living annual adjustment. Save the politicians some debating time.

So: when one of our elected representatives, state or national, *opposes* fair survival compensation for working Americans, remember the optionally tipped workers.

Visit these politicians in person if you can.

Then tip them a penny.

After Opening Night in Texas

Optional Theme: *Blood on the Saddle* (T. Ritter) **https://www.youtube.com/watch?v=qG5EqP1nyr0&ab_channel=John-Eagen**

The Bar had photos of Governor Abbott and DJ Trump everywhere, right next to the Confederate and Texas state flags.

These were fronted by colorful streamers and new **OPENING NIGHT** signs.

It was March of 2021, a year into the Covid-19 pandemic. The governor of Texas had declared, despite the deadly pandemic that still surrounded the city, that tonight bars, tattoo parlors, massage businesses, and *everything* else could be 100% open.

It looked like these could be the last months needed to follow the CDC safety guidelines. Anything else risked spikes in the pandemic, avoidable deaths for thousands. Didn't matter to the governor and his followers. They can pretend it's safe to celebrate NOW!

Human life here in this group of Texans was second to commerce. To profit. To stop the other political party, fresh in power, from success in ending the plague. To snatch defeat from the jaws of victory. Other states with similar leaders will follow this beginning- Wyoming, Mississippi, Alabama, Arizona, Oklahoma, Tennessee, more. All petri dishes for new virus mutations, some eventually vaccine-immune.

The bar owner, the governor's devoted follower and a major contributor, strode into his business only minutes before the 8 PM grand unlocking of the door. He held a box in his hand carefully as though it held breakable diamonds.

He signaled Sam, his security man, to stand by the door. Opening the precious box carefully, he confided: *"The governor himself sent me this. The very ones they use at his home."* So, smiling, he extracted a large thermometer from the governor's gift.

To his security man, he instructed *"Be sure you test EVERYONE who wants to enter, staff, dancers, or customers. Only the ones with NORMAL temps can come in. I'm no damn fool! And Sam: follow the instructions you find when you open the box. FOLLLOW THEM EXACTLY! Bonus if you do. Fired if you don't."*

With that the owner went home for a nap. A big night was expected.

At midnight he returned, rested, and brimming over with anticipation.

The bar was empty of customers. Furniture was broken, bottles smashed. A battered and bloody security man was the only one left.

"Sam! What's going ON here?"

Sam carefully pointed to the box at his feet. Crumpled and torn with blood stains.

He waved the instruction sheet and a stained thermometer between his bruised fingers.

He got out one word through broken teeth: *"Rectal."*

The owner sat on one of the few intact chairs and thought for a few minutes. Hard for him to do. His mother used to tease him when he did that: "*Anybody smell wood burning?*" she'd say. His father: "*He trying to think again? Lotta dumb in that boy!*"

Still, the owner did think some more, ominously, with Sam muttering "*What now?*"

Finally the owner smiled and stood.

"*Sam! We can always fix a few broken glasses and chairs, a few cuts and bruises. Don't you get it? Our governor knows that if everything opens, it gonna cause a huge Covid surge. Why thousands and thousands of celebrating Texans, and their friends in other places, all with no masks, no distance, no hand washing, no vaccine in their arms they all gonna die!*"

The owner thought again for a minute, choosing his words carefully. More for himself than for his damaged security man. He began again with more conviction. Maybe some pride. Louder.

"*I see it now. It begins here in Texas. But: NOT my little place, not me! He just wants me to be around still breathing when it's safe again. THEN I open! I'm one of the chosen ones for these End Times!*"

Sam stood silently waiting for the last of this. This guy could rationalize ANYTHING!

And here it came. The owner ended his thoughts even louder, prouder.

"*We may be the last bar standing in Texas but I will be rich. More rich. Where else can anybody go? Profits win! God bless the real and still President Donald Trump. Plus and especially our blessed Texas Governor Abbott. They saved me again!*"

And, leaving, "*Sam! Clean up and close up!*"

Cleaning up, including himself, took Sam until dawn.

Closing up was much faster. He had his severance money in his pocket from the bar safe. Had replaced it with his quit note and a receipt. Then washed his hands. Of all of it too.

Locking the front door, he put on his hidden mask, rubbed his left arm where the vaccine needle had gone, and decided to head home to ride out the coming storm.

He had been reading about Darwinism and the survival of the fittest. Maybe Darwin would aim his evolution at morons like his ex-boss. He hoped that all the good ones paying attention would be spared this time.

Hmm. To make that happen, Darwin might need some help. Sam could help.

Why not? Be on the surviving side with a real future?

We all had time now.

He walked free toward the Texas sunrise. Tipped his hat to it.

A Fast Descent in Rank

Optional Theme: *The Thrill is Gone* (B. B. King) **https://www.youtube.com/watch?v=oica5jG7FpU&ab_channel=NicolasReboux**

I was in the first class of the USAF OTS (Officer Training School) a slightly better alternative to being drafted which was likely in those days.

Before OTS, this program had been OCS (Officer Candidate School). OCS allowed for promotion to officer status up from the ranks while OTS required a college degree, thereby blocking promotions for Sergeants without said degrees. Something they might have been influenced by when they had merciless access to us in the training.

As the first of the newly constituted officer training cohorts we had undoubtedly more attention than those recruits in subsequent ones. Even Jimmy Stewart was there in his pressed Air Force General uniform along with some other assorted astronauts.

The first meeting of our orientation class was the most memorable, particularly for its candor. The fundamental MISSION of the US military was *"To Kill the Enemy"*.

The stated enemy there in 1962 was *"China"*. As one of the three large Asian Armies seen as *"threats"*. The other two were identified as North Korea and North Vietnam. In a quieter voice we were told that North Korea was at a stalemate, a kind of *"tie"*, so that *"for now"* our troops had at least neutralized that army and that need not be mentioned again. Lifetimes later not much has changed there, has it?

The STRATEGY then was said to be *"to take out the North Vietnamese army and encircle China"*.

Theme: *Ten Hours of the Imperial March (Star Wars/London Symphony Orchestra with John Williams)* **https://www.youtube.com/watch?v=FLgYVOTKrO8&ab_channel=10HoursChannel**

Simple and direct.

Especially 'simple' mentally. Sitting in that class and hearing this, I recalled that the legendary French Foreign Legion had been soundly defeated by the North Vietnamese ten years before. Not so easy!

Nor had this planned official Vietnam invasion started yet that year. The official Vietnam War had not yet begun. So the USAF as *"military advisors"* was going to fight North Vietnam alone?

At that time American troops or *"military advisors"* were said in the media to be there to *"liberate the Vietnamese people"*.

(Never mind that North Vietnam's leader, Ho Chi Minh, had earlier made genuine peace overtures to the USA, a country that he in principle admired.)

Yet here in this class, we had heard from some General Officers that the real strategic purpose of the invasion of Vietnam was to *quickly* defeat its army in order to next *"encircle China"*.

This invasion of a sovereign country at the sure loss of multitudes of lives on both sides was without moral or ethical justification. Worth dying for an injustice?

In the end, most of my training cohort would wind up dead or wounded in this misadventure.

At the end of training I had an opportunity to switch my career path to psychology graduate school. I took it. The commanding officer was enraged at my departure from an officer's career path and reduced my beginning rank from Staff Sergeant to Airman Basic (like an E-1 buck private in the army, or as low as you can get).

I held this bottom rank for my remaining six years in the Reserve.

Being married with three children, I couldn't be active reserve without being at a higher rank. I had been slated to be a Chaplain which intrigued me.

But when contacted, my former Commanding Officer refused to make the promotion.

So, being ineligible for active duty, I spent my graduate school years as a student with no active duty. No more marching.

I did become a psychologist. I am still officially at that lowest rank.

Best of all, I never invaded Vietnam.

Much later in the middle 1980s

I was chairing a psychology department in Pueblo, Colorado. Once a week I traveled to Colorado Springs to teach a psychology course to USAF students.

Walking through the frront gate in a three piece suit and tie brought about snappy salutes all along the way. I remembered that Generals often dressed that way and they were just making sure in case that was me. Besides, on the hierarchical rank chart, the top place, above the Commander in Chief, was for civilians, the people. Us.

The class was all military, no officers, and a pleasure to work with.

One day I walked into the full class to notice that there was precise chalk printing on the front board: **"This board will be fully erased at the end of the class."** It was signed by the base commander.

I told the class to consider this as a prediction, the base commnder's hypothesis. We then went on with another class session. At its end, I and the class paused to view the front board. I waited a minute, then another. Finally turned to the waiting class.

"No, he was mistaken. The Board was not erased."

The class cheered.

Chalk up another advantage for a top-of-the-chart citizen, even with the lowest rank.

A Little Bit More

Optional Theme: *Money* (Pink Floyd) **https://www.youtube.com/watch?v=cpbbuaIA3Ds&ab_channel=Arturo**

In 1980, a Safeway grocery chain store in San Diego made the national news. Somebody had left an extortion note on the shelves claiming that jars of their pickles had been poisoned. Other products too.

When the marked jar that the note was attached to was checked, the threat turned out to be true. The pickles were saturated with deadly poison.

No money was paid to the extortionist. The store manager had no way to know what else had been poisoned without testing virtually everything on the shelves. Beyond his authority. Nor did his authority allow for restocking everything and discarding all the store's food. It was decided at a higher management level to leave all the stock on the shelves and let the customers take their chances.

So the store was re-opened but with a large sign at the entrance warning customers that some of their purchases might be dangerous. The national publicity enhanced this warning. Much on the shelves was discounted to bargain levels. Ignoring the lethal danger, the customers showed up in larger than usual numbers. Their corporate business model had proved to be resilient.

At that time, the Safeway grocery chain motto was:

"All you could want in a store, and a little bit more."

Mister Jim Crow

Optional Theme: *Here Comes the Sun* (Sheryl Crow/George Harrison) **https://www.youtube.com/watch?v=99fDBasFpt8&ab_channel=CesarNakachima**

Robert Lee Green and I were walking from our plane in the Atlanta airport. Then the airport loudspeaker announced *"CALL FOR MR. CROW, MISTER JIM CROW"*. We laughed, knowing Jim Crow was exactly where we were.

"The term "Jim Crow" typically refers to repressive laws and customs once used to restrict Black Americans' rights, but the origin of the name itself actually dates back to before the Civil War. In the early 1830s, the white actor Thomas Dartmouth "Daddy" Rice was propelled to stardom for performing minstrel routines as the fictional "Jim Crow," a caricature of a clumsy, dimwitted Black enslaved man. Rice claimed to have first created the character after witnessing an elderly Black man singing a tune called "Jump Jim Crow" in Louisville, Kentucky. He later appropriated the Jim Crow persona into a minstrel act where he donned blackface and performed jokes and songs in a stereotypical dialect." –Evan Andrews

At this writing, Jim Crow describes the contemporary racial hostility exemplified by voter suppression, false arrests, police violence, job discrimination, and other dangers faced by Americans who are not Melanin-deficient whites.

This is also a time when so many have tasted more freedom than this, that there's no going back to the worst days of Jim Crow. Not having it. With some real work, a better future is within reach in the opposite direction. Can you see it? Here comes the sun.

A Cold Case Confession

Optional Theme: *Riders on the Storm instrumental* (Doors) https://www.youtube.com/watch?v=FNO4RXJvHZM&ab_channel=NamoRemixes

Pueblo Colorado 1976. I had no interest in being interviewed at the university newspaper. Not a time in my life when that was remotely important.

Still, when that day came I got ready to keep my word and be there. No time for breakfast. I filled a thermos half and half with split pea and beef barley soups. Not so creative thought a first time. They were the only soups available. The thermos and my empty stomach left for the newspaper building.

I was told the reporter was busy and would be late. Please wait in the first floor lobby. I sat. An hour went by. The thermos was empty. My stomach was singing- never a good sign. I didn't like the idea of just walking out. I did like the idea of not being there. Science reports that the stomach can influence our behavior, almost as much as the brain. Even has connections to the brain. It must have heard me. I sure was hearing it. Luckily I was alone in the lobby. The wind breaking was silent but lengthy. Impressive.

Soon there was a commotion from the upper floors. Then people began filing out the front door into the open air. One of them came up to me and said: *"We can't do your interview today. The building is being evacuated. They think it's a gas leak."* I left with relief. In more than one way. The next day's paper had a front page story, headed "**Whew!**", about the building evacuation. To them a mystery even to this day.

For me, a story to share with friends.

The Time Statue Song Game

Optional Theme: *For a few dollars more* (Danish National Symphony Orchestra) **https://www.youtube.com/watch?v=DT1NJwEi6nw&ab_channel=DRKoncerthuset**

This 21st century in-quarantine game became so popular it helped define the era.

Here's how it started

You are my Sunshine

Tony Soprano dares Paulie Walnuts to sing "You are my Sunshine" in his own words.

He complies, although he only knows a few lines.

"You are my sunshine, my only sunshine
You make me happy when skies are gray.
So don't you stiff me
For my fifty
Or I'll have to
Just blow you away."

Tony applauds and everybody joins in. Paulie scowls at first but bows, hiding his smile for after.

-

Summertime

Cardi B dares Megan Thee Stallion to make a short hot music video for them with this classic Gershwin song.

"Summertime and the weather is breezy
The fish are jumping
Cause the water is cold
Ooh wee ooh wee"

They both do a sexy freezing fish water jump.

It catches on across the country as the wiggly *Cold Fish Jump*.

When Cardi B came on James Corden's upbeat Carpool Karaoke segment, they did the *Cold Fish Jump*.

After that, a regular feature on his show was the *Time Statue Song Game*.

That's when it really took off.

-

Any Time You're Feeling Lonely

When Trevor Noah dared *Charlemagne the God* (Lenard McKelvey) to sing this but as existential psychologist Rollo May would have done so in therapy.

McKelvey easily rose to the challenge.

"Any time you're feeling lonely
Any time you're feeling blue
That's the time to remember
*That all **your** troubles came from **you**."*

Keenan Thompson on live TV was dared by Stephen Colbert to sing the *Anytime* song but to sing the *Anytime* song the way Anthony Fauci would sing it to Donald Trump.

He even threw in a little Oscar Brown Jr. too.

And sang this:

"Any time you're feeling lonely
Any time you're feeling blue
That's the time to remember
*That all **our** troubles came from you."*

In an Australian university in Singapore, we dared to sing this last existential version to an unpopular CEO. So some turnover followed, including me. But the point was made.

Appreciated too.

Things accelerated when on television Dave Chapelle dared Tina Turner to sing the song as Nine Simone but as she might have sung it to namesake revolutionary Nat Turner and as it would have been sung in the 19th century.

Tina rose to the challenge perfectly with her still youthful voice at its best.

Her Nina Simone version was chilling:

"*Any time you're feeling lonely*

Any time you're feeling blue

That's the time to remember

*That all **OUR** troubles came from **YOU**.*"

Count on Chapelle next to riptide the waters.

Soon his own mix-tape version became the theme for union strikes.

Next, it themed a few actual revolutions around the world against the dictators of many nations.

Much like the role music played in the end of apartheid in South Africa.

Climate Change wasn't the only change in the wind.

Optional Theme: *The Lion Sleeps Tonight* (Miriam Makeba) **https://www.youtube.com/watch?v=vdSg3dZSTDE&ab_channel=MiriamMakeba-Topic**

Miriam Makeba woke him up.

Whatever the contest was- he won.

Note for lawyers: Some of these events are speculative as they haven't happened yet.

Nor the next chapter either.

Boga

Optional Theme: *Havana (Gabe the barking dog)* **https://www.youtube.com/watch?v=qxfOjfM35dY&list=PL0T4yQB21YXk-bgnozjBMVZD4x6wdD6kOW&ab_channel=danimanz98**

"Yellow mustard custard dripping from a dead dog's eye" –Lennon/McCartney

In the mid-21st century, an exercise fad called *"Boga"*, or 'Bogus Yoga', suddenly swarmed over the climate survivor populations in various mountain caves. The most popular Boga exercise, by far, was the *"dead dog"* You lie on your back with all hands and feet straight up except for the fingers which were curled inward.

Music or song could include that Beatles line or the antique childhood 'four leaf clover' song: *"I'm looking over my dead dog Rover"*. This was ill advised to be done when the surviving large smart dogs were there. These shepherds, huskies, collies, retrievers, had been around humans so long that they would knowingly growl or worse during the Dead Dog exercise.

Now that the electronic age had been ended, there was a reversion with younger generations to what survivors could do on their own. This included a sardonic sense of humor and yet, hopefully, an ability to adapt. Hence: BOGA.

Note: Earlier in the century, the word 'BOGA' was also used for a wooden paddle board, a lizard, and the *Beyond Oil and Gas Alliance*. This last was a coalition to phase out a major greedy source of lethal climate change. Had it succeeded, civilization might have survived. Human survivors still remember that first BOGA with thanks for trying.

Columbus Perspective

Optional Theme: *The Godfather* (Nino Rota/Danish National Symphony) **https://www.youtube.com/watch?v=X-jdl9hcCeg&ab_channel=DRKoncerthuset**

Never having seen the starts, they deny the stars. Never having glimpsed the shining ways nor the mortals that tread them, they deny the existence of the shining ways as well as the existence of the high-bright mortals who adventure along the shining ways. The narrow pupils of their eyes in the center of the universe, they image the universe in terms of themselves, of their meager personalities make pitiful yardsticks with which to measure the high-bright souls saying: 'Thus long are all souls, and no longer; it is impossible that there should exist greater-stationed souls than we are, and our gods know that we are great of stature." Never having seen the mountains, there are no mountains. –Jack London 1916 (published 1986)

When I was in 3rd grade, we read that Columbus discovered America in 1492.

I raised my hand and asked *"What about the people already here?"*

"Those were Indians" said my teacher, *"but Columbus was a white man from Europe."*

I raised my hand again. *"I saw a man about to eat a sandwich in the park last weekend. He laid it on the park bench next to him and then started reading the paper. But when he reached for the sandwich it was gone. A hungry stray dog was eating it on the grass. The man was very angry at the dog."*

My teacher asked *"What is your point Robert? What did you learn from that?"*

I answered *"Well, I thought that the dog had stolen his sandwich and he was right to be angry. But now I realize that, like Columbus, the dog had just discovered that man's sandwich so it must have been okay to eat it."* She gave us recess early then.

(Response from Hans Toch: *"The moral is NEVER LEAVE YOUR SANDWICH ON A BENCH."*)

The Cultural Genocide Chart

Columbus killed and enslaved the indigenous people he encountered in his trips to the Caribbean: *In an era in which the international slave trade was starting to grow, Columbus and his men enslaved many native inhabitants of the West Indies and subjected them to extreme violence and brutality.*

On his famous first voyage in 1492, Columbus landed on an unknown Caribbean island after an arduous three-month journey.

On his first day in the New World, he ordered six of the natives to be seized, writing in his journal that he believed they would be good servants. Throughout his years in the New World, Columbus enacted policies of forced labor in which natives were put to work for the sake of profits.

Later, Columbus sent thousands of peaceful Taino "Indians" from the island of Hispaniola to Spain to be sold. Many died en route. Those left behind were forced to search for gold in mines and work on plan-

tations. Within 60 years after Columbus landed, only a few hundred of what may have been 250,000 Taino were left on their island.

As governor and viceroy of the Indies, Columbus imposed iron discipline on what is now the Caribbean country of the Dominican Republic, according to documents discovered by Spanish historians in 2005.

In response to native unrest and revolt, Columbus ordered a brutal crackdown in which many natives were killed; in an attempt to deter further rebellion, Columbus ordered their dismembered bodies to be paraded through the streets." https://www.history.com/news/columbus-day-controversy

History repeats these atrocities throughout the eras. In modern days, attention is increasingly being paid to the intergenerational trauma of the survivors.

Edison Uno was a professor at San Francisco State University and the California School of Professional Psychology. He was himself a survivor of WWII concentration camps for California's citizens of Japanese descent.

From this he lectured on the contrasting community survival strategies of subsequent generations of Chinese and Japanese Californians.

For the former, the strategy (facilitated historically by apartheid laws) was to cluster in "Chinatowns," maintaining language, culture, and safety.

For the latter, the strategy was dispersion, so much so that Uno observed

"If a Japanese American inhabits a home and the house next door is up for sale, another Japanese family will not buy the available home, will not live next door." (Uno, 1970, 1974, Uno & Maisie, 1992).

Facing hostile and dangerous ethnocentric forces, cultures have faced these challenges as charted here.

LEVELS OF CULTURAL CHALLENGE	
Annihilation	(Genocide, "Ethnic Cleansing," Holocaust))
Evacuation	(Deportation, "Removals")
Isolation	(Ghettos, Reservations)
Assimilation	(Cultural Removal)
Celebration	(Intact culture welcomed in larger community, gifts and differences appreciated)
These are listed in terms of greatest to least generational trauma, with only the last being a healthy outcome.	
I developed these categories for a lecture, following conversations with Edison Uno, and American Indian psychologist Arthur McDonald, when I was in my thirties.	
McDonald spoke directly after my presentation, beginning with this response:	
"The Cheyenne believe wisdom only comes with age. Wisdom is not likely before 60. When a man who has lived only 3 decades says something like this that sounds like wisdom, it is considered a coincidence."	
(McDonald 1978, Pond & McDonald 1997).	

–Robert F. Morgan

Note: In very recent years the federal holiday of *"Indigenous Peoples Day"* has taken the place of *"Columbus Day"*, a very welcome change reflected in the annual holidays of many states. Except for those states choosing to keep Columbus Day instead. Some of these also celebrate the federal *"Martin Luther King Jr."* holiday by sharing that day with a *"Robert E. Lee"* holiday. For some, yes, the past isn't even past. The rest step up to what can be a much better future.

Juneteenth Set Examples

Optional Theme: *It's a Family Affair* (Sly & the Family Stone) https://www.youtube.com/watch?v=xag5RKD0VHk&ab_channel=SlyATFamilyStoneVEVO

Juneteenth *is a federal holiday in the United States commemorating the emancipation of enslaved African Americans. Juneteenth marks the anniversary of the announcement of General Order No. 3 by Union Army general Gordon Granger on June 19, 1865, proclaiming freedom for enslaved people in Texas. President Abraham Lincoln issued the Emancipation Proclamation on January 1, 1863, freeing the enslaved people in Texas and all the rebellious parts of*

Southern secessionist states of the Confederacy.[25][26] *Enforcement of the Proclamation generally relied upon the advance of Union troops. Texas, as the most remote state of the former Confederacy, had seen an expansion of slavery and had a low presence of Union troops as the American Civil War ended; thus, enforcement there had been slow and inconsistent prior to Granger's announcement. The last enslaved people present in the continental United States were freed when those held by the Choctaw, who had sided with the Confederacy, were released in 1866.*

Inspiration for more modern times:

1. The more than two years delay before General Granger's message got delivered might well have inspired the long-lived DeJoy-led post office to slow down the mail.

2. Juneteenth was on June 19th but in 2022 was held on Monday June 20th, a day too late. Remembrance to General Granger.

3. The last line of this definition may have inspired Billy Joe McAllister to throw *something* off that Bridge on Choctaw Ridge. Then himself. Sad.

4. The slave owners got an extra two years of slavery by withholding the news of emancipation. These slaves were never compensated for this time. Today's corporate owners are inspired to emulate this event, at least by those very few who discovered this history, dared to copy it for their employees, but may not have a clue as to the meaning of the word "emulate".

Robert Lee Green & Martin Luther King: Revisited

Optional Theme: *Oh Freedom* (Golden Gospel Singers) **https://www.youtube.com/watch?v=Z5XaKmUsqoc&ab_channel=-GoldenGospelSingers-Topic**

To revisit this neighborhood in time, we remember an anthropological distinction made between the practice of *religion* and the practice of *magic*.

Religion is defined by a respectful gratitude to a higher power. Magic compels results from that higher power through ritual, formula, or sacrifice. Modern prayer can take both paths, prayers with thanks for blessings versus incessant prayers begging favors, even a winning game score.

A contemporary practice is termed *spirituality*. A version of this acknowledges the existence of higher powers, internal (human potentials) or external, and respects any gift from that source as freely given, deserving of appreciative gratitude.

That distinction between thanks and demands can apply on a human level.

Especially when we can acknowledge those who have done so much to protect and improve our existence. When in the presence of such wonderful hosts, we should thank them, freely, for all their profound hospitality. This chapter is meant to do exactly that.

Understanding our key past events requires providing more attention to these two courageous pioneers, one far too unknown and the other celebrated now as a National Holiday in his own country. Maybe today's world is the best time to remember what they contributed then.

Dr. Robert Lee Green_

Who led the visit to the Union of South Africa that sparked the economic boycott that ultimately ended Apartheid and freed Nelson Mandela to begin Reconciliation?

Who co-wrote with Martin Luther King Jr. the speech to the American Psychological Association that reshaped modern Community Psychology?

Who was the only full time psychologist working with Dr. King, and so closely that he was one of the six bearers of Dr. King's coffin?

Who was the African American psychologist who planted the American flag on Jeff Davis's Confederate monument? Who was the African American psychologist from Detroit to stage a sit-in protest against a barber shop owned by people with black skin who would only cut the hair of people with white skin?

When an entire county in Virginia closed its schools for four years to avoid desegregation, who took on the research to follow these thousands of children, re-open the schools, identify critical periods for learning, and develop an empirical basis for seeing measured intelligence as environmentally dependent?

Is this the same psychologist who helped found and develop Head Start along with Follow Through in the US (and *Newstart* in Canada) as well as modern schools of urban studies or special education or desegregation institutes?

Yes, and his name is Dr. Robert Lee Green, now a retired President of the University of the District of Columbia, author and professional speaker. Today living in Nevada with his wife Lettie, children grown and away.

I met Dr. Green on the Human Relations Committee of the city of East Lansing, Michigan. He had recently graduated from Michigan State University with a doctoral degree in Special Education and had been hired as a young Assistant Professor. When he attempted to buy a home there for his young family, he was told that the realtors had a written prohibition against selling property in their city to anybody of Dr. Green's race. As usual, Bob did not accept this: whenever faced with the alternatives of bad and worse, he always generated a third choice.

He went with me directly to the university president. Now this president, John Hannah, had been appointed by President Eisenhower as National Chair of the United States Human Relations Commission. He did not want an embarrassment in his own back yard.

President John Hannah's academic background was essentially a B.A. in Poultry Science enhanced by marriage to the prior university president's daughter. He also had many high level friends in the national Republican Party. In record time he had substantial funds rolling in from other countries, international students, parents, governing families, and corporations developing resources for the growing war in Vietnam.

Hearing of Green's housing dilemma, Hannah called the Chair of the MSU Speech department (who was also the Mayor of East Lansing). The university president ordered him to put a Human Relations Committee together to look into Dr. Green's situation. Not to resolve it exactly, but definitely to consider it carefully, or at least publicly. While this phone call was being held, I noted a huge painting on President Hannah's wall depicting slaves picking cotton.

In any case, the Commission was formed. Besides Bob there were eight other members, seven of which were friendly to the realtors. The last and ninth seat was held open for a student at Michigan State University: that was me. I earned this seat because I was the only volunteer from MSU's 30,000 students – not a selection particularly based on merit.

As the press-covered public monthly meetings progressed in City Council seats, the other Commission members agreed that Bob had been treated unfairly. Yet they argued for change by persuasion instead of a new law. They stated that we needed to create positive community change by changing attitude rather than behavior. A classic argument resolved usually by existential context or *"it depends"*. In this clear case of injustice, attitude change alone as a first approach of course did not work.

It took Green and me half a year to get them to (barely by a vote of 5 to 4) move to behavioral change, let attitude follow, and to ask the City to pass a law ending racial discrimination in East Lansing. How we did this is another story but it borrowed heavily on the work of a Social Psychologist, Solomon Ash.

Dr. Green then took me under his wing and allowed me to bootleg an unofficial second pre- and post-doctoral internship with him that involved special education, innovative federal poverty programs, and assisting Dr. King in the last four years of King's young life.

Green's work on the vulnerability of measured children's intelligence made him famous, leading to changes in educational patterns in the USA and in Bermuda among other places. His Prince Edward County, Virginia, project included the organization of Martin Luther King Jr. who took Dr. Green on as his key Director of Citizen Education. Responsibilities included Adult Literacy programs in Chicago, Desegregation Institutes across the country, and innovative educational methods in and out of government throughout the world (Green *et al* 1964-1969, 2015; Morgan 1969, 2012, 2018).

It was Robert Lee Green who went to the apartheid Union of South Africa with Arthur Ashe and other African-American celebrities to see for themselves what actually was being done there. Mandela was in jail and the press was censored. Green, Ashe, and the others received intense criticism from both left and right political figures for what they charged seemed implicit support of a rogue apartheid regime. But just as Mandela had been doing from his cell, Green was studying the opponent, knowing that information-based decisions were more effective.

It was Green that noted that the apartheid regime would fail without the continued economic support of some very visible western corporations. Not that these corporations responded immediately or willingly, but a broad-based economic sanctions campaign was launched to withdraw university and union retirement funds from any corporation doing business with South Africa's regime. Eventually this worked, along with a growing (and music-influenced) rebellion by the mistreated South African majority in-country. With economic sanctions, racial rebellion, and a fear of a bloodbath, only Mandela and his Reconciliation plans held hope to the white leadership for a non-violent transition. Mandela was released and history tells the rest of his successful story.

Dr. Green now consults internationally here and there, but he chides me for assuming he's *"still only 35 years old"*. He no longer looks like a young Denzel Washington. He looks like an older Denzel Washington (smile).

Psychologist Green remains largely unknown to the public. Well, not well known enough. If only more people knew of the national and international legacy of his lifelong applied decades of contribution to assessment, community psychology, the organization of Black Psychologists in the American Psychological Association, special education, urban psychology, and the career launching of younger psychologists like myself.

Well, with great good fortune, I know him.

And now you know him too.

Dr. Martin Luther King Jr.

September, 1967. Martin Luther King Jr., was only 38-years-old but already president of the Southern Christian Leadership Conference, and winner of the Nobel Peace Prize when he stepped to the microphone, not something he really needed, at the American Psychological Association (APA) Annual Convention in Washington, D.C.

Robert Lee Green and I collaborated in the development of this speech, suggesting some paragraphs, a few of which he approved. I learned later that Ambassador Andrew Young had said that he contributed separate input as well. When addressing a specific professional group, Dr. King always wanted to review what this group was all about, their issues and goals, so he could build an informed speech around core ideas that were entirely his own.

Dr. King never needed a ghost writer. Or a teleprompter. He was always on top of delivering his own speech, his own principles, and his own powerful delivery. Bostonian and calm at first; louder, faster tempo, and more emphatic in the middle; with powerful impact for the close. The few sentences we suggested seemed reasonable but kind of mundane. To listen to what he ultimately delivered was hearing a script brought to life from this great orator. The speech was moving, persuasive. Even to an auditorium full of psychologists.

A re-reading of his powerful address today captures the urgent tone of the 60s, as he cajoled the nation's social scientists to 'tell it like it is', to invite them to join a crucial and just cause. In fact, to APA's membership, whom he addressed as *'concerned friends of good will,'* his plea for help in changing a society *'poisoned to its soul by racism,'* seems now much more poignant in light of the tragedy of his death that struck only seven months later.

My minor portion and Green's went to him through a meeting Robert Green had with King. I was honored to see if anything we suggested had met with King's approval, and fit his message for that day. What a lifetime gift to contribute any part of this. The words he spoke that Sept. 1, as the convention's Invited Distinguished Address, were reprinted in the *Journal of Social Issues* (Vol. 24, No. 1, 1968).

Whenever you read it, please use your auditory imagination to hear him speak it. And if you can, see him on that stage in this everlasting live statue in time.

While the speech was in galley proofs, the shocking and numbing news of his assassination was released.

Another time statue

It was 1964 in Atlanta, Georgia. Thanks to Robert Lee Green, it was time for my first visit to the main office of Martin Luther King Jr.

At age 23, still a graduate student, I anticipated meeting this older man in his late thirties. Now I was just outside his Southern Christian Leadership Conference (SCLC) office entrance.

From the street I could see, just beyond the front door, was a woman at her reception desk. She was white. This I learned later meant racists were far less likely to shoot into the office as, at that time, such women were held in some esteem by gun loopy white supremicists. Some. Maybe. Also from the street, I could see another office just past her on the side, still very visible. That was where Dr. King worked, where I would be with him shortly. Once inside, the receptionist told me that the other SCLC leadership and staff had offices not in any direct line from the front door or street.

The layout was "L" shaped with the receptionist and Dr. King in the smaller leg of that "L", the only ones in line from any bullets fired from passing cars. The rest were housed in the more secure larger leg of the "L". Not that they stayed there for long.

I wondered what kind of human family member, clearly lacking conscience or sense, would shoot into an office building in downtown metropolitan Atlanta and still expect to have no consequences. Maybe dimwit ones who might do a drive-by shooting from a bus?

In his office

Dr. King was ready to see me.

I entered his office. Stepping from behind the desk, he shook my hand. His hand enveloped mine like a glove, reflecting the welcome in his voice. I was a head taller at 6"4" than the older man but he seemed much larger, seeming to fill the room.

Green had told me of King's athleticism. I could see for myself that he was solidly built and, in his thirties, at his prime. All the more remarkable that he was truly nonviolent.

Most others around him bought into nonviolence as their own strategy to achieve equity and justice. Not King. He lived it. I thought of him in later years when the best martial artists shunned fighting anywhere outside exhibitions.

We sat in comfortable chairs and spoke together for an hour. In that time, outside the content of our conversation, I noticed that he effortlessly sat like a King, deserving his last name.

There began my four year study of his regal posture, nonverbal leadership confidence, speaking tone shifts, and fully focused attention on whoever he was spending time with. What was it about this man, our human family cousin, to endear him so completely to those of us whose path he crossed? Existentialists might say it was his clear righteous purpose in life, a primary mission he was willing to die for. And did.

Coming from Buffalo, I grew up with an excessive disdain for celebrity. Even earned celebrity. I had also as a child lived across from a very lively Black church, amazingly beautiful in its own powerful way (the music!), but run by a Black minister who was also the local slumlord exploiting families fresh up from the South. I at that time shared my father's distrust for clergy of all races. Yet here I was in the presence of our most celebrated clergyman. He was the real thing, genuine, driven. I trusted him instantly.

With no tact whatsoever, I asked him what he thought of Robert Williams, a Black veteran whose gun club with other Black veterans was achieving initial success at desegregating parts of the South. Williams had a perspective that was the antithesis of Dr. King's. Williams threatened retaliation for injustice, freedom by strength. Wasn't this more congruent with the American spirit than the Asian Indian nonviolent approach of Gandhi?

King was patient and gracious in his response, explaining nonviolence as though I had just recently discovered it and could use some tutoring. In fact I did. What a fine teacher.

(The success of Williams ended when Freedom Riders came through, bringing after them cowardly white racists who expected no pushback from nonviolent people. They fired into residential homes randomly. To their surprise, Black veteran gun club members fired back. The battles ended with Williams a federal fugitive fleeing the country, labeled a dangerous "paranoid schizophrenic" by a local Sheriff.)

We spoke about our families. He was truly energized by this. I asked him about the SCLC stress tests. For example, if they were to get to the airport in an hour in order to catch a plane, they would leave half an hour late and do their best. At least once a plane had stopped in mid-runway to let King and the reverends on. He laughed and said it wasn't so much of a test as it was his continual oversight. But, on reflection, he could see that it was good preparation for handling crises. Of which there was no shortage.

Dr. King's resume or CV was only a few pages long but ended with a paragraph, very important to him, about his wife and children. Right after the listing of the Nobel Peace Prize.

Toward the end he spoke about my working at SCLC, even part-time as I was, assisting Dr. Green. He said he never made an important organizational decision without first listening carefully to each of his staff. Each one was heard out. Once that was done he would consider fully everything that had been said. In the end though, much as King deserved his name, the decision would be his alone. The deciding factor would not be a majority vote or the persuasion of friends. It would be *"the right thing to do"*.

This was exemplified by the discussion around whether he should go beyond his desegregation efforts, for which he had the full support of President Johnson, to move forward on economic justice or equity.

Even more controversial was the choice to oppose the war in Vietnam, an intrusion into a Civil War involving the invasion of another country. This had tragic consequences that included the deaths of thousands of young Americans as well as the Vietnamese defending their own country. Yet, that would lose President Johnson's support completely, also magnifying the right wing hatred for King already led by J. Edgar Hoover's FBI. Consequences could be deadly. Almost all staff advised against these initiatives, especially the Vietnam one. Robert Lee Green was an exception, supporting this antiwar direction. (I wasn't at this meeting but through Bob I was another exception.) King reflected quietly. Silence. Then he announced that he would do the right thing. They moved ahead on all these initiatives.

In Michigan, the desegregation marches had not been molested. The police kept order and did their jobs. Years later, the anti-war in Vietnam marches had a different reaction. Police clubs came out, protesters arrested in great numbers, generations highly divided. By 1968, Dr. King had been murdered. He died doing the right thing.

Once my 1964 conversational hour with Dr. King was over, I met with Green and went to work. Program evaluation, desegregation institutes, an Adult Literacy program in Chicago, suggestions for speeches, whatever could be contributed.

This while and after finishing my doctorate in Michigan, an internship at Hawaii State Hospital, globetrotting consultations or site visits for government programs with Robert Green, and a young family of five to support. Very full and very enriched four years.

Never again did I get a one-on-one with Dr. King before the four years and his life ran out. We both had been very busy, particularly him. Bob Green was a great observer though, always keeping me informed, involved, aware.

Dr. King's verbal and nonverbal leadership never let up. Dr. King's was the first "Rainbow Coalition", insisting on a place for all races in his staff and in the movement.

I studied his command of a room, confidence in his goals and in all of us. On stage in a panel or on TV, he sat alert and focused. Should a staffer have an urgent message for him, he would keep looking forward, tilt his head slightly so the staffer could whisper the message in his ear without his shifting focus from forward. Regal. Effective.

Positive Psychology challenges clinicians to define the opposite of all those diagnostic categories. What can be at the other end of the human potentials spectrum? What would a totally healthy person, mentally and physically, be like?

Probably somebody athletic, compassionate, loving, eloquent, with a great sense of humor, a generous spirit, decisive, inclusive, definitely a higher primary purpose for living as a reason for gladly beginning each day as a gift.

Who always jumps to my mind is Dr. Martin Luther King Jr.

And yes, definitely, Dr. Robert Lee Green as well.

Chapter end optional theme: *Amazing Grace* (Golden Gospel Singers) **https://www.youtube.com/watch?v=vcE0b_dddXY&list=RDvcE0b_dddXY&index=2&ab_channel=GoldenGospelSingers-Topic**

Bonus

The advent of our former president in 2016-2020 may have been foretold in this 1955 precognitive book:

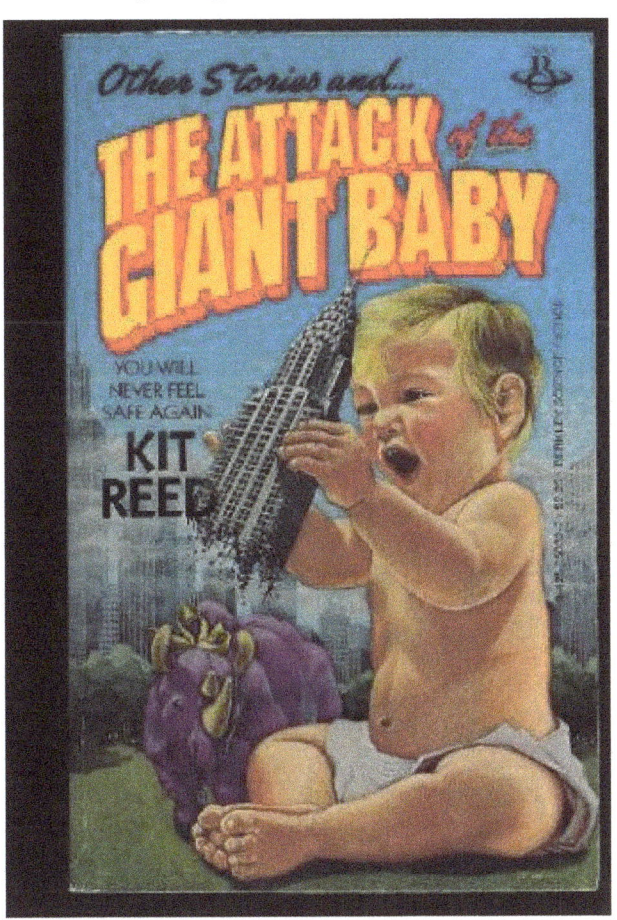

Hope for the Next Generation

Theme: *A Change is Gonna Come* (Sam Cooke) **https://www.youtube.com/watch?v=fPr3yvkHYsE&ab_channel=EntreCielEtTerre**

Well, that would be a change. Our children would seem to be inheriting a world in its final days. Planet heating toward extinction, war growing ever more lethal, even nuclear soon. Pandemics spreading. Dictatorships multiplying, democracies diminished, division ballooning.

You know the list.

At the time of this writing, maybe all those now militarily acknowledged UFOs, from the future, deepest ocean, or elsewhere, are all just here to witness this dramatic extinction.

So how about some light on the remote possibility that the human family can somehow unify at this last moment and surmount these threats. Open a path to a better future. Survive.

There is a memory that might on a very small scale predict such a possibility.

Fresno, California, in the 1980s

Fresno is next to some great national parks and some high polluting billion dollar agriculture.

The huge rural region around Fresno was then a magnet for Vietnam resettlement refugees and a continuing migration of interracial workers from Mexico and points farther south.

One of my graduate students, Bradford Chang, was doing his doctoral dissertation with me at a professional psychology school there. It was on what psychology can contribute to special education for students in diverse cultures. As part of this work, he was doing his internship in a nearby rural Head Start drawing migrant children from these cultures.

He asked me to join him there and help where I could. I agreed.

Brad worked, quite skillfully, with the children. I found a role by meeting every week with their parents.

To do this, I received the help of four translators. Spanish of course. Also Vietnamese, Laotian, and Hmong.

The parents often began with seeking advice for their Head Start child but, as most had large families, questions soon refocused on the other children. On calls for help to parents dealing with their child's behavioral issues

I brought in aspects they might not have received from other places.

Based on David Cheek's hypnosis work, I suggested that at the end of each day the parents quietly stop in the sleeping child's bedroom, sit, and gently thank them for anything helpful; or successful that they might have done that day, even by mistake. No complaints though. Just the positive.

I was given some authority here as a credentialed professor, which in these cultures mattered much more than we were used to. So they tried it out and it worked. The behaviors improved.

As the weeks went by, I noticed that the Laotian translator took much longer than the others. It became increasingly clear that he was adding his own improvisations.

A parent who was bilingual met with me and the Laotian translator to sort it out. Mostly the translator's improvisations were reasonable and we soon precluded any more of what wasn't.

The Hmong questions soon moved from children to daily life. These had been mountain people living in basic rugged conditions. Now living in California they had need to sort out the use of a bathtub with a faucet providing running water. I thought it creative when they filled the tub with soil and planted crops that could be irrigated from the faucet. Some other more experience parents clarified the usual alternative option.

From the start, the parents sat in five different clusters. Little or no friendship occurred between clusters. Even some near hostility between a few.

I was often busy trying to have a more unified parent group but no luck.

The North Vietnamese and the South Vietnamese were particularly antagonistic to each other and sat in opposite corners of the room.

The Laotian parents formed their own closed group, discussing their own children's progress.

The Spanish-speaking parents too stayed focused only on their own children's issues, not much on other culture's parents whose languages made communication out of reach.

All seemed to look down on the Hmong and ignored these parents though I found the Hmong to be the most effective at using whatever

I suggested. Or, for that matter, what the other Hmong parents had found to work. The Hmong parent group was best at growing as a mutual helper group, one that would continue long after Head Start ended. An important goal.

Brad meanwhile had worked very well with the Head Start staff and children. Tests showed enhanced intelligence, improved educational skills, learned content, and enhanced emotional well-being.

In our supervision sessions, he shared an important observation. None of the children were clustered like their parents. The budding friendships crossed all cultural lines. By the end of the Head Start experience, they all seemed happy, friendly, cooperative, and ready for public school next year.

At my last session with the parents, I shared this information. They all seemed pleased with the success of their children. But I decided to ask.

Why were they still so divided against the other cultures in the room when their own children, at such a young age, succeeded at group unity?

Each of the translators explained this to me until all parent cultures were represented. For once there was agreement.

This was not their original country. They had no interest in making peace outside their own. They saw themselves as fully formed, either with no interest or no ability to change much. Though they would try, they thought they were too old to adapt more than they had to. (Wrong.)

But they had learned here that the main job of a child was to learn how to survive where they were. They were in California now. A very new home.

The children were acknowledged as being at an age where they would be best at adapting. Being unified across cultures was what was done here.

So be it.

The parents saw their children as the future of their family. Each parent said they fully supported friendships and play dates across culture. For their children.

Not for themselves.

They now knew the next generation would survive then.

Their children would adapt as survivors always did.

It was now expected.

Brad became Dr. Chang in 1989.

Departures

With love for the many now departed friends including Josette Mondanaro, Tom Crowley, Bert Karon, Hans Toch, Stephen Johnson, Becky Crockett McGuane Fonda and Peter Fonda, Stuart Twemlow, Ben Camo, Nathan Hare, and my forever sister Pat Norman. Time Statue artists all. If I left anybody out, well, I wish you had waited longer.

Some of the more recent departures will be remembered here.

Ernst Beier, Ph.D.

Optional Theme: *The Sounds of Silence* (Simon & Garfunkel) https://www.youtube.com/watch?v=4fWyzwo1xg0&ab_channel=SimonGarfunkelVEVO

His life's giant contribution was about reading our silent body language.

An international psychology division for the American Psychological Association (APA), now Division 52, was originally the idea of a small group led by Ernst Beier, eventually its first President. I recall Fran Culbertson and Florence Denmark particularly among the several distinguished advocates for international involvement leading our initial charge.

We were longtime veterans of the process. I've been in APA since 1966 but I was far from the oldest in the group. I got to be the first awards coordinator, dividing the award categories between USA and non-USA recipients.

In all of this Ernst was the catalyst for progress as a leader that never seemed to tire.

His two decade age advantage over me and most of the rest of us was clearly an example of the vitality and accomplishment some psychologists keep to the end of a very long life.

Always charming and universally appreciated, Ernst epitomized what I call the Golden Rule of Proportionality: he solved far more problems than he created.

Maybe moreso than most others I have known, he was always at his best.

An international psychologist pioneer, Ernst Bier, was a celebrated expert on body language. His popular book *"People Reading"* was a best seller. His *"The Silent Language of Psychotherapy"* was a key volume for therapists.

His day job was as a psychology professor in Salt Lake City, Utah.

In the summers he would travel to exotic locales like New Guinea, following the cultural variations of body language there. He also enjoyed sailing, skiing, trekking, traveling, visiting and interviewing shamans, and piloting his own plane.

Not bad for man then in his eighties.

When I met Ernst, he looked a lot like the mustached man about town in the *Esquire* magazine.

On the other hand, he spoke with a strong German accent. Add to that his military history in World War Two, and my first erroneous impression was that he had fought on the Nazi side.

As we got to be friends, I asked him how he reconciled that experience. He seemed startled. No, he was on the *American* side.

The German accent? What accent?

In fact Ernst had been a Jewish refugee, immigrating as a young man to America and fighting as soon as he could *against* the Nazis. He had joined the US Army, Tenth Mountain Division, but was sent overseas with the 28th Infantry division. He was captured at the Battle of the Bulge by the Germans and survived a POW camp. After liberation he received the silver battle star.

Now a Jewish professor in a predominantly LDS university?

"*Exactly!*" he confirmed with a broad smile.

A few years later, he was my invited keynote speaker at a professional psychology school graduation in California.

Ernst and a restless audience waited for his turn through about an hour of preliminaries.

When I finally could introduce him, I reviewed his outstanding body language contributions briefly. Much of that was beginning to appear in television series and in books on poker tells.

I told the already restless audience that if they had read his books, they would have been able to follow his speech already. Since while he was waiting he had given it sitting there on the stage silently twice now. (Laughter.)

Now awake, they were focused. Actually, once using actual out loud spoken words, he gave a fine talk. Lots of insights graduates could use.

Still with a great German accent though.

Until suddenly he was no longer there. Or anywhere. Nobody that I asked knew.

There was a rumor that Ernst, now in his late 90s, had Alzheimers. Or, my initial favorite, that he had run off to New Guinea to be with a tribal woman.

One day I finally succeeded in tracking his phone number down and called. Frances, his wife of 65 years, answered.

Once she knew who I was, she apologized: *"I'm sorry. Ernst is bedridden now. At 99 years old, his mind is fine but he no longer can speak. You can talk to him on the telephone but he can't answer you. There's not much time. We are told he won't live out the week."*

If only I could see him. Then I knew he would answer me just fine without speech.

But I took what I could in the time we had, being thousands of miles apart.

I talked one-way for a while, reminding him of past good times, funny twists in our life, and wishing I could be there to enjoy his stories, even if by body language.

When I was done, his wife took the phone again.

She said: *"He's smiling now"*.

Pat Norman

Optional Theme: *Amazing Grace* (B. Obama) https://www.youtube.com/**watch?v=IN-05jVNBs64&ab_channel=C-SPAN**

*"**Pat Norman** began her activism in California in 1971, when she founded the Lesbian Mothers' Union to address and defend child custody issues for lesbians. In 1972, she became first openly gay person hired by the San Francisco Department of Health to serve the gay community. She was a key leader in the development of AIDS care, called the San Francisco Model, which involved a collaborative network of city agencies, community organizations, hospitals, and healthcare providers. Norman was a lecturer and consultant to nonprofit and public agencies from 1974–1988, and was the statewide director of training for the Youth Environment Study (YES), Inc., from 1988 to 1989. She was a co-chair for the California State Mobilization for Peace, Jobs, and Justice, 1984; co-chair of the National March on Washington for Lesbian/Gay Rights, 1987; a delegate to Jesse Jackson, Democratic National Convention, 1988; a member of the Nelson Mandela Reception Committee, 1990; and a*

co-chair of the Stonewall 25 Organizing Committee, 1994, where demonstrators unfurled a one-mile-long, 30-foot rainbow-colored flag symbolizing lesbian and gay rights. Roughly one million participants from around the world converged on the Avenue of Americas in New York City on that day. Norman was founder, president, and chief executive officer of the Institute for Community Health Outreach, an organization that provides training for community health workers, especially focusing on underserved and stigmatized populations. She retired in 2002, and shortly thereafter moved to Kauai, Hawaii, where she lived for 20 years. Throughout the years, Norman also served on several public commissions: the Police Commission, Fire Commission, and the Human Rights Commission. She provided years of leadership on nonprofit boards such as serving as the president of the Black Coalition on AIDS, the president of SAGE (Standing Against Global Exploitation), and the president of Larkin Street Youth Center. Pat Norman was portrayed by Whoopi Goldberg in the docuseries When We Rise, which was released in early 2017." – San Francisco Bay Times, August 11, 2022

Death brings the curtain down on a life story in progress. Each of us creates our own story day to day, moment to moment. Statues in time, always there in that place, that time. Often the end is far too soon. Pat Norman's first born son, Paul, died in a car crash just as his story turned from turbulence toward a happier path with love for his wife, children, family, friends. Martin Luther King Jr had his life story ended before he ever turned 40. So much accomplished in that little time but what if he had lived at least twice as long? Such interruptions can be profoundly hurtful to those of us who had been included in that ongoing life. The more powerful their story, the greater this departure is a loss to our own. Pat Norman had the time to earn a fortunate outcome, fortunate for all the lives she touched, fortunate for the freedom and care of many generations. In San Francisco's creative non-traditional early 1970s, Pat and I heard from several sources that we had been twins in an earlier life. While this might not have been literally true, it fit us very well. From then on, we became brother and sister. Since we each periodically had been raising children on our own, now the two families came together. The children had both of us in their corner. As we got older, many of them were in our corner. It was of course somewhat of a shock to Pat's mother, Maude, when she visited and learned she had birthed a 230 pound man she didn't know about. Pat lived more than twice as long as Dr. King, like him she accomplished much for the human family as well as her own. Wish their life story had gone on at least as long as ours. Well Pat, what a story it was. Be at peace now. And hear our applause.

ROBERT F. MORGAN

Hans Toch, Ph.D.

Optional Theme: *Time Keeps on Slipping/Fly Like an Eagle* (Steve Miller)**https://www.youtube.com/watch?v=6zT4Y-QNdto&ab_channel=chinita41**

Hans Toch, an original pioneer in the fields of social psychology with emphasis on criminology and criminal justice, died June 18 2021 at his home in Albany, New York.

Born April 17, 1930 in Vienna, Austria, he escaped the ravages of the holocaust, initially to Cuba and then to the United States. He earned his B.A. at Brooklyn College in 1952 and his Ph.D. in psychology at Princeton in 1955.

He served in the U.S. Navy, and was a Fulbright Fellow in Norway, a visiting Lecturer at Harvard, and a member of the psychology department at Michigan State University before being recruited in 1967 as a founding faculty member of the School of Criminal Justice at the State University of New York at Albany, the first program in the country to confer the Ph.D. degree in criminal justice.

Professor Toch remained on the faculty at the University at Albany until his retirement in 2008, attaining the rank of Distinguished Professor and mentoring countless students and junior faculty members over the course of his lengthy tenure.

His scholarship reflected a consistent humanistic bent and a concern for representing the viewpoints, understandings, and humanity of the subjects of his writings: offenders, police officers, the incarcerated, and correctional officers.

He authored more than 30 books including such classics as *Violent Men: An Inquiry into the Psychology of Violence*; *Living in Prison: The Ecology of Survival;* and *Stress in Policing*. He received the August Vollmer Award from the American Society of Criminology in 2001, and in 2005 he was recognized with the *Prix DeGreff* award for distinction in clinical criminology by the International Society of Criminology.

He was a fellow of the American Society of Criminology and of the American Psychological Association, and in 1996 served as president of the American Association for Forensic Psychology.

Sixty years ago I was an undergraduate student in Hans Toch's classes at Michigan State University. I liked his regular two courses so much that I next enrolled with a friend in his personalized special studies research class.

Our student contributions included interviews with Malcolm X and an explorative diagnosis of the Socialist Labor Party.

Over the next decades, his own contributions revolutionized the field. A decade later in 1978, I published a debate with Bernard Diamond and others on the Insanity Defense, a book completely inspired by Hans.

By then we were longtime friends and colleagues. Turned out that we had ancestors from the same parts of Eastern Europe, so much that eventually Hans declared that we were likely related and I was his *"Homie"*.

His reviews of my work that followed stood out for their clarity, brevity, and insightful humor. My favorite was the close of his cover quote for my *Iatrogenics Handbook* (2005) on the doctor's mistakes: *"If the shoe fits, it will hurt"*.

He eventually said he experienced his own share of iatrogenic medical mistakes, declaring that he was at the end of his road and that his home was his hospice.

We next spent eight years still exchanging ideas, until I began to doubt his demise was likely after all, at least not in this century.

But he was bound to be right eventually. And as usual, in 2021, he was. Glad he waited at least as long as he did.

What a dear friend, gift, genius, and guide he was to me in this chaotic world. What a fine mind and unforgettable sense of humor.

He certainly loved his wife, children, and friends. It is returned.

In tribute to his brilliant sense of humor and dialogues with his students, I close with a quote from one of my Canadian students, a nurse.

In my *Iatrogenics Handbook* (page 447) she recommended a surgery that might be applied to those lacking a sense of humor or with *Novumnotiophobia** (unrealistic fear of new ideas) or *Novumlibrophobia** (overwhelming fear of books that are new or unusual) as follows: *"The Optoectomey severs the cord connecting the eyeballs to the rectum, thus eliminating a certain negative outlook on life."*

I followed her suggestion next with the last sentence in the book:

"May we all enjoy life to its fullest, cords and balls intact." Hans sure did.

References

Optional Theme: *Sleepwalk* (Ritchie Valens) **https://www.youtube.com/watch?v=iSIUUmFHg18&ab_channel=CassianoPastori**

Arnold, W. (1955,2017). Shadowland. San Francisco: Berkley.

Barch, A.M., Ratner, S.C., & Morgan, R.F. (1965) Extinction and latent reacquisition. *Psychonomic Science*, 3, 495-496.

Bar-Ilan University (2018) "Forging a quantum leap in quantum communication: Scientists introduce a technique that speeds up quantum information processing nearly a million times." *Science Daily,* 9 February. <www.sciencedaily.com/releases/2018/02/180209112342.htm>.

Battino, R. (2006) *Expectation: the very brief therapy book*. Norwalk, CT: Crown.

Bickford, J. (2002) *Delancey Street Foundation: American Dreams*. Las Vegas, Nevada: American Dreams.

Bloudoff-Indelicato, M. (2013) Beaver butts emit castoreum goo used for vanilla extract that the FDA regards as "natural flavoring". *National Geographic* (10).

Brandt, D. (1973). *Play Therapy with Adults: Effects on Child Rearing and Self Concept*. Ph.D. dissertation, California School of Professional Psychology, San Francisco.

Breggin, P.R. (1994) *Toxic psychiatry*. New York: St. Martins

Breggin, P.R. & Cohen, D, (2007) *Your drug may be your problem*. New York: HarperCollins.

Bütz, M.R. (1997). *Chaos and complexity: Implications for psychological theory and practice.* Washington, D.C.: Taylor & Francis.

Bütz, M.R. and Schwinn, R. (2004) "Transforming Crisis Theory in Behavioral

Healthcare: Moving from stasis to developmental adaptation." Paper presented to the Society for Chaos Theory in Psychology and the Life Sciences, Marquette University, July *16*, 2004.

Cheek, D. B. (1968) *Clinical hypnotherapy*. New York: Grune & Stratton.

Cheek, D.B. (1993) *Hypnosis: the application of ideomotor techniques.* New York: Allyn & Bacon.

Cheek, D. B. & L. LeCron (1968) *Clinical hypnotherapy.* New York: Grune & Stratton Consortium for Longitudinal Studies (1983) *As the twig is bent: Lasting effects of preschool programs.* Lawrence Erlbaum: Hillsdale, New Jersey.

Davidson, A. (1999). *The Oxford Companion to Food.* Oxford University Press. p. 263.

Elkind, L. (1972) *Effects of hypnosis on the process of aging.* San Francisco, CA: California School of Professional Psychology. Unpublished doctoral dissertation.

Elkind, L. (1981) Hypnotic intervention: Elkind's contribution. Chapter 2 in R. F. Morgan *Interventions in applied gerontology.* Toronto: Kendall/Hunt, 33-58.

Elkind, L. (2017) Personal communication.

Green, R.L. & Morgan, R.F. (1969). Effects of resumed schooling on the measured intelligence of Prince Edward County's Black children. *J. Negro Educ.* 38, 147-155.

Hoehn, A.J. & Woolman, M. (1969) Operational context training in individual technical skills: ED041233. . Clearinghouse for Federal Scientific & Technical Information: Springfield, Virginia.

Karon, B.P. & VandenBos, G.R. (1981). *"Psychotherapy of Schizophrenia: Treatment of Choice."* New York: Aaronson.

Kozol, J. (1967, 1985) *Death at an Early Age: The Destruction of the Hearts and Minds of Negro Children in the Boston Public Schools.* NY: Houghton-Mifflin, Plume.

Kozol, J. (2006) *The Shame of the Nation: The Restoration of Apartheid Schooling in America.* New York: Three Rivers Press.

King, M.L. *(*1964, 1981) *Strength to Love.* London: Hodder & Stoddard (1964), Minneapolis, Minnesota: Augsburg Fortress (1981).

Lazar, I., Darlington, R., Murray, H., Royce, J. Snipper, A., & Ramey, C.T. (1982) Lasting effects of early education: A report from the Consortium for Longitudinal Studies. *Monographs of the Society for Research in Child Development, 47 (2/3),* 1-151.

Levitt, H. Frost, D.M.M., Bamberg, M., Creswell, J. W., Frost, D. M., Josselson, R., & Suarez—Orozco, C. (2018). Qualitative and mixed methods research standards. *American Psychologist, 73* (1), 26-46.

McDonald, A. (1977) Personal communication. Pueblo, Colorado.

Mondanaro J. (1989) *Chemically Dependent Women: Assessment and Treatment.* Lexington, Mass: Lexington Books.

Morgan, R.F. (1964a). The adaptational behavior of chicks in a spinning environment. *Psychological Record, 14,* 153-156.

Morgan, R.F. (1964b) *Uncas Slattery/ The Muddy Chuckle.* New York: Exposition. (1987 version a two-act play.)

Morgan, R.F. (1968). Need for a greater use of efficiency percentages to supplement reports of statistical significance. *Perceptual & Motor Skills, 27,* 338.

Morgan, R.F. (1978). *Should the Insanity Defense be Abolished?* (With William Carnahan, Bernard Diamond, Eugene Turrell). National Judicial College and the Nevada Division of Mental Hygiene & Mental Retardation Proceedings, Reno: Human Services Education.

Morgan, R.F. (1982) Balloon therapy. *Canadian Psychology,* 23, 45-46.

Morgan, R.F. (1983) Community dispersion or problem resolution? Hypothetical plight of community residential patients with appendicitis. *Psychological Reports, 53,* 353-354.

Morgan, R.F. (1999). *Electroshock: the Case Against.* (With Peter Breggin, Leonard Frank, John Friedberg, Bertram Karon, Berton Roueche) Albuquerque, NM: Morgan Foundation, 1999. (Chapter IV reprinted in Brent Slife's *Taking Sides: Psychological Issues, 13th edition,* Guilford, CT: McGraw-Hill/Dushkin, 2004 and in Richard P. Halgin's *Taking Sides: Abnormal Psychology, 2nd edition,* Guilford, CT: McGraw-Hill/Dushkin, 2002. (First edition: *Electric Shock.* Toronto: IPI Publications, 1985.)

Morgan, R.F. (2005a). *Training the Time Sense: Hypnotic & Conditioning Approaches* (With Linn Cooper, Elizabeth Erickson, Milton Erickson, Gary Marshall, Christina Maslach, Paul Sacerdote, & Phillip Zimbardo.) Albuquerque, NM: Morgan Foundation.

Morgan, R.F. (2005b). *The Iatrogenics Handbook: A Critical Look at Research & Practice in Helping Professions.* (With Robert Alexander, Peter Breggin, Jeffrey Buck, David B. Cheek, Juanne Clarke, Frank Epling, Stanley Fevens, David Frey, John Friedberg, Glen Gabbard, D'Arcy Helmer, Lenore Jacobson, Mark Kamlet, Richard Mason, Michael Miller, Geoffrey Nelson, Carl Rogers, Robert Rosenthal, Jalal Shamsie, Thomas Szasz, Benjamin R. Tong, Stuart Twemlow, Kenneth Walker, J.B. Woodward). 456 Pp., Albuquerque, NM: Morgan Foundation. (1st edition: Toronto: IPI)

Morgan (2012). *Trauma Psychology in Context: International Vignettes and Applications from a Lifespan Clinical-Community Psychology Perspective.* Santa Cruz, CA: Morgan Foundation.

Morgan (2021) *Time Statues.* Santa Fe, NM: Winds of Change Press.

Morgan, R.F. & Toy, T.B. (1970). Learning by teaching: a student-to-student compensatory tutoring program in a rural school system & its relevance to the Educational Cooperative. *Psychological Record,* 20, 159-169.

Morgan, R.F. & Elkind, L. (1972) National Institute of Mental Health Children's Community Mental Health Center Grant for the John Hale Health Foundation, National Medical Association, Bayview-Hunters Point, San Francisco. Empowerment model: Coordinated by single-parent interns for their own children and for prevention intervention with community children.

Morgan, R.F. & Toy, T.B. (1974) "Learning by teaching: A student-to-student compensatory tutoring program and the educational cooperative." In J.G. Sherman (Ed.), *Personalized System of Instruction (PSI) Germinal Papers: Selected Keller Plan Readings.* Menlo Park, CA: W.A. Benjamin, Inc., 1974, 180-188.

Moulon, R. & Morgan, R.F. (1967) Sibling bondage: A clinical report on a parricide and his brother. *Bulletin of the Menninger Clinic,* 1967, 31, 229-235.

Pond, D. & McDonald, A.L. (1997) *Cheyenne Journey: Morning Star, Our Guiding Light.* Santa Ana, CA: Seven Locks Press

Neill, A.S. (1978) *Freedom-not license!* London: Pocket.

Neill, A.S. & Lamb, A. (1995) *Summerhill School: A new view of childhood.* New York: St. Martin's Griffin.

Reich, W. (1981) *Record of a friendship: The correspondence between Wilhelm Reich and A.S. Neill 1936-1957.* New York: Farrar, Strauss, Giroux.

Roach, M. (2021) *Fuzz: When Nature Breaks the Law.* New York: Norton.

Rogers, R. (2011) *Destiny's Landfall: A History of Guam.* Honolulu: University of Hawaii Press.

Roske, Allan. (1984). *Predicting Violence in a Maximum-Security Penitentiary: A Matter of Survival.* Ph.D., California School Professional Psychology, Fresno.

Rossi, E.L. & Cheek, D.B. (1994) *Mind-Body therapy: methods of ideodynamic healing in hypnosis.* N.Y.: Norton.

Segal, R. (2016). "The Case for a Central Patient Portal for Medical Records". *Huffington Post*, 31 August. https://www.huffingtonpost.com/entry/the-case-for-a-central-patient-portal-for-medical-records us 57c5e17de4b07addc40f87ba

Seneca (65BCE, 2004) *On the Shortness of Life: Life is Long Enough if You know How to Use It*. New York: Penguin.

Shaked, Y., Michael, Y., Vered, R.Z., Bello, L., Rosenbluh, M., & Pe'er, A. (2018). Lifting the bandwidth limit of optical homodyne measurement with broad-band parametric amplification. *Nature Communications, 9* (1).

Sherman. J.G. (1974) Learning by teaching: A student-to-student compensatory tutoring program and the Educational Cooperative". In J.G. Sherman (Ed.), *Personalized System of Instruction (PSI) Germinal Papers: Selected Keller Plan Readings*. Menlo Park, CA: W.A. Benjamin, Inc., 1974, 180-188. Reprinted from the 1970 publication in *The Psychological Record*.

Shapiro, J. (1970*). Investigating the effectiveness of sensitivity training of nurses on the progress of their patients.* Unpublished PhD dissertation at the University of Waterloo, Ontario, Canada.

Simard, S. (2021) *Finding the Mother Tree: Discovering the Wisdom of the Forest*. New York: Knopf Doubleday.

Slattery, U. (2005). *Unfortunate baby names: Slattery's complete collection of the most notable ten thousand for dramatic or other usage*. N. Charleston, SC/Grass Valley, CA: Morgan Foundation.

Toch, H. (1980) T*herapeutic communities in corrections*. New York: Praeger.

Toch, H. (1995) "Inmates involved in prison governance." *Federal Probation*, 59, 34-39.

Toch, H. ((1997) *Corrections: A humanistic approach*. Albany, N.Y.: Harrrow & Heston.

Toch, H. (2017) *Violent Men: An Inquiry into the Psychology of Violence*. 25th Anniversary Edition. Washington, DC, American Psychological Association.

Uno, E. (1970) *Hearings relating various bills to repeal the Emergency Detention Act of 1950*. Washington, D.C.:United States. Congress. House. Internal Security.

Uno, E. (1974) *Concentration camps, American-style: racism greed and hysteria led to concentration camps*. San Francisco: San Francisco State University.

Uno, E. & Maisie, R. (1992) *Executive Order 9066: The Internment of 110,000 Japanese Americans*. Berkeley, CA: University of California, Asian American Studies Ctr.

Von Uexkull, J. (1957). A stroll through the worlds of animals and men. In C.H. Schiller (editor) *Instinctive Behavior*. New York: International Universities. 5-80.

Wohlleben, P. (2018) *The Hidden Life of Trees: The Illustrated Edition*. Vancouver, Canada: Greystone.

Wohlleben, P. (2019) *The Secret Wisdom of Nature: Trees, Animals, and the Extraordinary Balance of All Living Things — Stories from Science and Observation (The Mysteries of Nature, 3)*. Vancouver, Canada: Greystone.

Woolf, N.H. & Silver, C. (2018) *Qualitative Analysis Using MAXQDA*. New York: Routledge.

Woolman, M. (1967) *Basal progressive choice reading program*. Atlanta: Institute for Educational Research.

Robert F. Morgan

Born in the lull between the two world wars, he now shares his lifespan perspectives on today's interesting times with us.

Robert F. Morgan, Ph.D. is a Life Member of the American Psychological Association. An NIMH Pre-Doctoral Fellow at Michigan State University, he continued with more than 60 years of post-doctoral practice and teaching experience.

A former speech collaborator and project consultant for organizations including Dr. Martin Luther King Jr., he was founding editor of the Cambridge University Press Journal of Tropical Psychology, and founder of the Division of Applied Gerontology in the International Association of Applied Psychology (IAAP). He has overseen 126 psychology doctoral dissertations in California, Singapore, and Australia, along with a contemporary trauma psychology seminar at the University of New Mexico. He has published more than a hundred articles and 17 books on topics including life span psychology, trauma psychology in context, applied gerontology, international psychology, and even unfortunate baby names.

Only semi-retired, he avoids a lethargic status by continuing to think and write. He also hopes to avoid that opposite error exemplified by misleading voices of our era and, of course, Lincoln's prescient warning: *"It is better to be silent and thought a fool than to open one's mouth and remove all doubt."*

Well, his readers will continue to be the judge of that.

Optional Theme: *Peter and the Wolf instrumental* (New York Stadium Symphony Orchestra) **https://www.youtube.com/watch?v=Fmi5zHg4QSM&ab_channel=NewYorkStadium-SymphonyOrchestra-Top**

Other Books by Robert F. Morgan

Time Statues

Trauma Psychology in Context: International Vignettes and Applications

Opportunity's Shadow & the Bee Moth Effect: When Danger Transforms Community

Growing Younger: How to Measure & Change Body Age

The Iatrogenics Handbook: Research & Practice in Helping Professions

Training the Time Sense: Hypnotic & Conditioning Approaches

Unfortunate baby names: Slattery's complete collection with the most notable thousands for dramatic and other usage

Electroshock: the Case Against.

Directory of International Consultants in Psychology

Interventions in Applied Gerontology

Measurement of Human Aging in Applied Gerontology

Should the Insanity Defense be Abolished?

Conquest of Aging: Modern Measurement & Intervention

The Effective Verbal Adaptation (EVA) test: Parts A & B

The Educational Status of Children in a District without Public Schools: CRP 3221.

The Educational Status of Children during the First Year Following Four Years of Little or No Schooling: CRP 2498.

Uncas Slattery and the Muddy Chuckle

www.ingramcontent.com/pod-product-compliance
Lightning Source LLC
Chambersburg PA
CBHW041139110526
44590CB00027B/4070